A CLOUD OF WITNESSES
CREATIVE PEOPLE OF THE BIBLE

A Cloud of Witnesses
Creative People of the Bible

WILFRID HARRINGTON O.P.

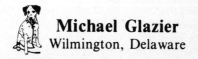

Michael Glazier
Wilmington, Delaware

ABOUT THE AUTHOR

Wilfrid J. Harrington is an Irish Dominican. He is Professor of Scripture at Dominican House of Studies at Tallaght and the Milltown Institute of Theology and Philosophy. He is also lecturer in the School of Hebrew, Biblical and Theological Studies at Trinity College, Dublin. His most recent publications include *The New Guide to Reading and Studying the Bible*; *Mark*; *Jesus and Paul: Signs of Contradiction*; and *The Drama of Christ's Coming*.

First published in 1989 by Michael Glazier, Inc.,
1935 West Fourth Street, Wilmington, Delaware 19805,
by arrangement with Gill and Macmillan Ltd., Dublin.
© 1988 by Wilfrid Harrington, OP

Library of Congress Cataloging-in-Publication Data

Harrington, Wilfrid J.
    A cloud of witnesses.

    Bibliography: p.
    1. Bible—Biography.   1. Spirituality—Biblical
teaching.   I. Title.
BS571.H24   1989   220.9'2 [B]   89–24623
ISBN 0-89453-747-4

Printed in Great Britain.

Cover design by Pinnacle, Dublin.

In Memory of
Agnes
my Mother

CONTENTS

Pilgrim Spirituality

Excursus. Biblical Spirituality: An Irish Dimension

INTRODUCTION:
Pilgrim Heroes and Heroines

Spirituality is one of those ultimately undefinable terms. Religious orders, for instance, lay claim to distinctive spiritualities. The claim is not hollow. But the spirituality is easier to experience than to define. As a Dominican I am conscious of a 'spirituality'—perhaps it might be termed an ethos—which I, instinctively, recognise. But, please, do not ask me to describe it. In practical terms, spirituality is recognisable in the lives of individuals and of communities. For, if 'spirituality' does not find issue in life-style and conduct it is surely spurious.

There is a biblical spirituality. Rather, given the refreshing pluralism present in Israel and in the early Church, there are spiritualities. The 'saints' of Israel and of nascent Christianity are the exponents. And it is they who will enable us, tentatively at least, to essay a broad definition of spirituality. Its source is an experience of God, an experience that cannot remain lonely dialogue with God. There must be a reaching out to people. It might seem that, in some Christian traditions, this latter dimension is absent. What about hermits, or the strictly enclosed religious orders? Paradoxically, such withdrawal from the world, if it be authentically Christian, is an expression of concern for the human race. An inspiration of such spirituality is a conviction of the power of prayer. In the Catholic tradition a dramatic verification of this insight has been the designation of a Carmelite nun, who never stirred beyond her convent walls, as patroness of missionary endeavour: Thérèse of Lisieux.

In our look at the biblical picture we will have to do with people who, in all cases, all of them, made some impact on their surroundings. To be quite accurate, one should say, rather: they are presented as so doing. The truth is, not a few of our heroes and heroines are either wholly fictional or, while historical, are painted with creative abandon. It is the story

1

that matters; happily we are rediscovering the power of story. We turn, then, to the story characters to discover and illustrate our biblical spiritualities. Perhaps, at the close, we may discern a pattern and recognise that there is, after all, a broad biblical spirituality.

In view of the fact that the Old Testament covers four-fifths of our Christian Bible, it is no surprise that Old Testament people will be numerous in my pages. They have been chosen—there had to be a stringent selection—not on grounds of importance alone but also because they are interesting. And they have been chosen irrespective of fictional or historical status. We will find striking and, I hope, pleasing contrasts. For instance: Abraham and Jacob, Amos and Hosea, Ezekiel and Qoheleth. We will hear some straight talk addressed to God from Jeremiah and Job. We will meet the earthy Samson, the gentle Ruth and the formidable Judith. A goodly company, of saints—and of sinners. Men and women of faith—if, sometimes of rude faith. They speak to us of God, a God of humankind. They bring us hope.

My New Testament people are more predictable. If we take seriously the designation hero and heroine, there are those who cannot be left aside on any showing. The Baptist, Mary of Nazareth, Paul—they *must* appear. I will argue that Mary Magdalene should, on no account, be omitted from the shortest list. The evangelists raise something of a problem because we know them only through their writings. Yet, they cannot be set aside. And, without doubt, the Hero *par excellence* has to figure.

The third part seeks to draw the stories together under the separate, but related, headings of pilgrimage and spirituality. I hope that, here, the pattern of the book will become clear. While, at surface level, it looks like a series of brief sketches, two unobstrusive threads have run through it. When they are knotted, at the end, the parts are gathered into a unit.

The series is meant to have an Irish dimension. In the matter of the Bible that dimension could be supplied readily enough. We become more and more aware of a period of intense study of the Bible in the early Irish monastic schools (roughly AD 500–850). Besides, there is an abundance of early *Lives* of Irish saints. The material was there. The question was: how to avail of it. I might have fitted related anecdotes into my biblical sketches—but that could lead to confusion. Then, Seán de Paor came to my aid and readily agreed to contribute an appropriate Excursus. I here formally thank him.

He has brought out, unmistakably, an Irish preoccupation with pilgrimage. And he has made clear that the Irish monks had taken the Bible to heart. Throughout the book we will have seen something of the liveliness of biblical story. Now we will get a taste of exuberant Celtic imagination. A lovely trait is an affection for the animal world—reflected elsewhere in the bizarre, but always attractive, animal population of the Book of Kells. The Irish have ever been wanderers; and they have always been story-tellers. And they have had a taste for the things of God. In these areas they are not unlike the children of Israel.

Wilfrid Harrington, O.P.

The
Old Testament

THE BEGINNING

It is always helpful to begin at the beginning. The first eleven chapters of Genesis are, unarguably, a beginning and, arguably, the most theologically important area of the Old Testament. What emerges from these chapters is the centrality of creation. What emerges, too, is the sheer goodness of the Creator and the goodness of creation. That divine goodness realistically accepts that humankind will resent the limitation that has to be an essential feature of humanness. Humankind is the summit of God's creation. In man and woman God has his image—his counterpart. With humankind alone, among all his creatures, can he have dialogue. Because he is a loving God, that dialogue must be free. His counterpart will respond to him in freedom—or not at all. As a realistic God he accepts that humankind will constantly abuse freedom, will seek to go it alone. The related stories of Genesis 2:4b-3:24 and 11:1-9 make the point. The truth is, our God is divinely inconsistent. He never does follow through his threats. Just look at his record over a few chapters.

'... of the tree of knowledge of good and evil you shall not eat, for on the day that you eat of it you shall die' (Gen. 2:17).* We go on to hear that the man and woman did eat of the tree—but they did *not die*! (3:6). Surely, we would think, a murderer like Cain had forfeited life; instead, his life is protected: 'the Lord put a mark on Cain lest any who came upon him should kill him' (4:15). In face of universal human corruption God declares: 'I will blot out man whom I have created from the face of the ground...for I am sorry that I have made them.' Fine—except that 'Noah found favour in the eyes of the Lord'! (6:7-8) Even when it comes to the arrogant civilisation of Babel, the scattering over the face of the earth blends into the call of Abraham and a new beginning (11:1-9; 12:3). God always backs down. Why? Because he is the God who, when it came to it, did not spare his own Son. He would and did take that desperate gamble. Because that was his intent

*Quotations from the Bible are taken from *The Holy Bible, Revised Standard Version*, London: Nelson 1959.

from the beginning, he will stick with humankind to the bitter end. Our hope could be that, as Creator, he might have the last word. Our confidence is that as our Father, he will have the last word—in his way and in his time. In the meantime he would have us march in pilgrimage towards his goal for us. His only wish is that we get there.

God has created humankind free and responsible. The biblical record shows that humankind has been consistently disobedient. What resulted is an ongoing struggle—dialogue is too tame a term. God is too respectful of humankind to settle only for polite dialogue. He wants his counterpart to talk back when needful. And Israel obliged! We will see examples of unabashed candour. Sadly, Christianity seems to have lost that Hebrew knack. Our God loves a good scrap. There is the precedent of Jacob!

A Promised Land

A fascinating feature of the religious history of Israel is the fact that not until near the beginning of the second century BC was there any notion of an after-life. Of course, there was Sheol. But that abode of the dead is nothing other than the grave where all—good, bad and indifferent—ended up indiscriminately. We find, then, that the hope and vision of Israel were set firmly within *our* world of humankind. That it took so long for Israel to reach an acceptance of real life beyond death can, to a Christian, be a shock and a scandal. How could it be that God's chosen people were unable to see beyond this world to the world of God? Instead of causing upset, that fact might well be a salutary reminder to us that our world *is* world of God. Here, and not anywhere else, is where we live and move and have our being. We become what we are meant to be by wholly accepting our humanness, not by any vain attempt to deny it. It is ironical that the Old Testament, without encounter with God-made-man, can point out for us so much more clearly the way of authentic humanness than do many trends of historical Christianity.

The Creator had given his earth to humankind as a sacred trust. It could not be otherwise in the gift of the land to his people. The land demanded respect; it must have its sabbath rest (Lev 25). This provision was much more than agricultural common sense. It was a constant reminder that the land was gift and that the land had its rights. And the weekly sabbath had its place in this context. It was an institutional reminder that frantic human endeavour is not an indispensable need. The world will not end if the people take time to acknowledge their God and his saving deeds (Ez 20:8-11); Dt 5:12-15). Neglect of the sabbath, as Amos clearly saw, could only lead to abuse of the land and exploitation of the people of the land. Sabbath and religious festival were, to the landed, waste of valuable time—time that might be more profitably spent in squeezing the poor (Am 8:4-6).

The most pressing obligation that went with possession of the land was care of the poor, the sojourner, the widow and orphan—all those without possessions. They are truly 'brothers and sisters', participants in the covenant promise (Lev 25:25-55). That there will be needy ones is a realistic acceptance of the human way: 'for the poor will never cease out of the land' (Dt 15:11a). Response to the situation is a solemn duty of the graced heirs of the promise: 'Therefore I command you, you shall open wide your hand to your brother, to the needy and to the poor, in the land' (15:11b). The prophets were unsparing in their castigation of the exploitation of the poor: it was callous thanklessness, gross betrayal of the covenant. And, at the end, it was the poor ones, the *anawim*, who would end up being heirs of the promise: 'Blessed are the meek, for they shall inherit the earth' (Mt 5:5).

Biblical faith is firmly linked to land: the land of Israel, the land of Galilee and Judea. The covenant of Yahweh and Israel is about land: about promise and possession and threatened loss of land. Israel lived in the hope of a gift, in enjoyment of gift, and in its loss by treating gift as something that belonged of right. Jesus would insist that the Kingdom is gift, to be received only by one who could receive it gladly as a child does. The gift of God is ever held in trust. And failure in trust will ever lead to loss.

9

NOAH—*and his Flood*

Every so often an expedition sets out—usually from the USA—to Mt Ararat, in search of the remains of Noah's ark. I can imagine no more futile project—compounded by the fact that Ararat is a region (exactly where, we are not sure), not a specific mountain. Such expeditions bring home to one how literalism can ruin the finest story. I have recently, in another context, observed that we have three Christmas stories: those of Matthew and Luke and then *our* Crib story, an amalgam of them. The biblical Flood story offers a close parallel. When one analyses Genesis 6:5-9:17 one can readily unravel the text and come up with two very nearly complete and distinctively independent Flood stories: one, the older Yahwistic story; the other a later Priestly version.[1] But the existing Genesis text offers a third form of the story which is not a slipshod scissors-and-paste operation but a sophisticated re-presentation. The fact that one can identify three, notably different, forms of the Flood narrative ought to point us in the direction of right discernment. We Westerners will persist in putting the wrong question to story or, at least, to biblical story: is it true? did everything happen just as related? Any Semite hearer of the story (and our biblical stories are culturally Semitic) would ask: what does it mean? And that, of course, is the right question. We are annoyed by disturbing inconsistencies in biblical story. A Semite will shrug his shoulders and say: what the heck! It is the meaning of the story that matters—not unimportant details. More about that.

An Older Noah

I have noted three Genesis flood-stories. The fact is: flood-stories are worldwide, cropping up in the most diverse cultures. For the biblical scholar the most interesting of them have to be Near Eastern stories—especially those of Meso-potamian origin. Here it will be enough to indicate one of them: the flood-story from Tablet XI of the Assyrian-version Gilgamesh Epic. Gilgamesh was legendary king of Uruk in Mesopotamia; accounts of his adventures are very early indeed. The clay tablets which contain the Epic in its Assyrian form were discovered during excavations in Nineveh, in the ruins of the library of the last great Assyrian king, Assurbanipal. During his travels, Gilgamesh had encountered Utnapishtim the Faraway—the Babylonian Noah. And Tablet XI of the Epic is Utnapishtim's own account of the flood. It is a story remarkably close to the Yahwistic biblical story and not notably different from the Priestly version. There can be no doubt that the biblical narratives are distinctively Israelite forms of much older and widely distributed Near Eastern stories.

Another Ark

In the Gilgamesh story we are told: 'In those days the world teemed...and the great god Enlil was aroused by the clamour.... "The uproar of mankind is intolerable and sleep is no longer possible by reason of the babel." So the gods in their hearts were moved to let loose the deluge.' This is remarkably like: 'The Lord saw that the wickedness of man was great on the earth, and that every imagination of the thoughts of his heart was only evil continually...I will blot out man whom I have created"' (Gen. 6:5, 7). Again, where the god Ea betrayed the design of the gods to Utnapishtim, 'Noah found favour in the eyes of the Lord' (6:8). Next, in each case, the building of an ark; the Babylonian vessel being vastly the more impressive. Each ark was destined to preserve 'the seed of all living life'. Then the Deluge, so awful that 'even the gods were terrified at the flood, they fled to the highest heaven...they crouched against the walls, cowering like curs'. When the flood had done its work—'all mankind was turned to clay'—the boat grounded on Mt Nisir. Utnapishtim loosed three birds: a dove, a swallow and a raven—the third did not return because she had found dry land. Finally, a lavish sacrifice for the gods: 'when the gods smelled the sweet savour, they gathered like flies over the sacrifice'. And they agreed that there would not be another flood. Surely, we have to do with a basically common story. The next expedition that sets out in search of Noah's ark might have a look for Utnapishtim's boat—a much more noble craft!

The Utnapishtim flood-story is only one of many flood stories, some very old; others have been passed on orally to our

11

day. Each, it seems, reflected an event confined to a limited geographical area. Especially in regard to the older stories which look to the beginning of human history, a universal flood would seem to be an excessively uneconomic way of dealing with a small human population! What is at issue is an awareness that the human race is open to threat: a feeling reinforced by natural disasters like earthquake and volcano—and disastrous floods. Let us recall the shockingly destructive floods in Bangladesh not many years ago.

It Grieved him to his Heart

When we turn to the Genesis flood stories we note, at once, that the polytheistic atmosphere of the Babylonian story is absent. God is wholly in charge and the flood offers no threat to him. Still, there is in common the idea that even the Hebrew God could be capable of destructive action: all reality was ultimately traced to God or the gods. But even here is the great difference: the grief of Yahweh. 'Yahweh was sorry that he had made man on the earth, and it grieved him to his heart. . . . I will blot out man whom I have created from the face of the ground' (6:6-7). The sorrow and grief are not acknowledgment of a bad mistake in creating humankind in the first place; they flow from Yahweh's observation that 'the wickedness of man was great in the earth, and every imagination of the thoughts of his heart was only evil continually' (6:5). This means wholesale corruption—to such a degree as to threaten human existence. God *has* to do something about the situation. Hence the 'inconsistency'. The first decision, 'I will blot out man', is followed by the statement: 'Noah found favour in the eyes of the Lord' (6:8).

The conclusion of the Yahwistic story (8:20-22) is Yahweh's abrogation of his decision to destroy. 'I will never again curse the ground because of man (a reference to 3:17—"cursed is the ground because of you") neither will I ever again destroy every living creature as I have done' (8:21). Not that he is under any illusion: 'for the imagination of man's heart is evil from his youth' (8:21b). God has decided to put up with humankind's tendency to evil. One is reminded of Mathew 5:45—'For the Father makes the sun rise on the evil and on the good, and sends rain on the just and the unjust'. An interesting point is

God's reaction to Noah's sacrifice: 'Yahweh smelled the pleasing odour' (8:21)—echo of a phrase in the Gilgamesh story. There we noted the rather sickening picture of gods swarming like flies over the sacrifice. Here it is metaphor: God has graciously acknowledged Noah's sacrifice.

The Rainbow

If the Yahwistic story ends with sacrifice, the Priestly story, not surprisingly, closes with covenant (9:8-17). Noah was no priest and sacrifice was a levitical prerogative. The Priestly story simply could not close with illegitimate sacrifice. The 'covenant' is God's self-commitment: '... never again shall there be a flood to destroy the earth' (9:12). God goes so far as to tie a string around his finger! He not only makes a promise but gives the assurance that he has included a built-in reminder: 'I set my bow in the cloud, and it shall be a sign of the covenant between me and the earth' (9:13). A gracious touch.

Before the covenant there was renewal of the blessing of 1:28-30. 'And God blessed Noah and his sons, and said to them, "Be fruitful and multiply, and fill the earth"' (9:1). It is an assurance that human life and destiny will continue after the Flood. But there is tension in the new world. Before (1:28-30) there was harmony—there were no carnivores! Now it is no longer a matter of human dominion over the animal kingdom—now creatures go in fear and dread of humans (9:2-3). How prophetic—as destroyed and threatened animal species have discovered.

The Third Story

So far I have referred to the original biblical Yahwistic and Priestly flood stories. What we find in our Genesis text is a third story, woven of the two. And the new story has a drift and a point beyond either. It is fascinating to see how the editor has proceeded. He has made little or no attempt to iron out discrepancies. Thus, the cause of the flood and its duration vary conspicuously. We have noted the different endings: sacrifice and covenant. In this respect the animal manifest is revealing: 'And of every living thing of all flesh, you shall bring two of every sort into the ark, to keep them alive with you; they shall be male and female' (6:19—Priestly). 'Take with you seven pairs of all clean animals, the male and his mate; and a pair of the animals that are not clean, the male and his mate' (7:2—Yahwistic). Why the difference? Because the Priestly story ends with covenant, a pair of each species is enough. The Yahwistic story ends with sacrifice (which demanded 'clean' animals). If there had been only a pair of all, then certain species were finished! The story takes care to provide an abundance of sacrificial animals. In short, while the Yahwistic and Priestly stories are each internally consistent, the compiler of story three is sublimely unconcerned by inconsistencies in detail. That is because he is more concerned with his message.

The editor has given the story a fresh shape. And he has given it a very firm centre: 'God remembered Noah' (8:1). That verse is a watershed—if one may be forgiven the pun! Just look at the sequence: violence (6:9-10), resolution to destroy (6:13-22), command to enter the ark (7:1-10), the flood (7:11-24); *God's remembrance of Noah* (8:1), receding flood (8:1-14), command to leave the ark (8:15-19), resolution to preserve order (8:20-22), covenant blessing and peace (9:1-17). Up to 8:1 there is a movement towards chaos—but a remnant is saved. After 8:1 there is a movement towards a new creation with Noah and his family as seed of a new humankind. It is a powerful new story; a more firm message of promise and hope.[2]

The later Noah
Noah figures in later biblical tradition—notably in Sirach and Wisdom. Among the famous men of old, 'Noah was found righteous ... everlasting covenants were made with him' (Sir 44:17-18). In Wisdom Noah is one of those guided by wisdom—wisdom saved the earth from total destruction, 'steering the righteous one by a paltry piece of wood' (Wis 10:4). Noah would not have been amused at that description of his splendid boat! Hebrews 11 is closely parallel to Wisdom 10, except that now the Old Testament saints had been guided by *faith*. Because Noah had heeded God, 'he condemned the world and became an heir of the righteousness that comes by faith' (Heb 11:7). In 2 Peter 2:5 Noah is characterised as 'a herald of righteousness'. And, in 1 Peter 3:19-21 the salvation of Noah in the midst of water is presented as a type of salvation through the water of baptism. Rather forced, one must admit.

Still, it does make the valid point that salvation is always God's doing.

Conclusion

What has the flood narrative to say to our day? If it is true that behind every flood story is the awareness that the human race stands under threat, then the narrative may indeed have relevance in our nuclear age. Apart from threat of nuclear war there is the menace of another and more frightening Chernobyl. True, our God has solemnly promised that *he* will not devastate the earth. But he is sadly aware that 'the imagination of man's heart is evil from his youth'—*we* might do the job, quite effectively. I, for one, will always find my comfort in the assurance: 'Noah found favour in the eyes of the Lord ... God remembered Noah'. God *will* have the last word.

ABRAHAM—*Man of Faith*

Abraham was chosen and called—the 'scandal' of divine election. He was called to serve the divine purpose and in this service the scandal is resolved. Abraham was summoned to break with all natural ties: country, clan and family (Gen 12:1). He was to get up and go—'to the land that I will show you': the demand on his faith is radical. The author of Hebrews has a perceptive comment: 'By faith Abraham obeyed when he was called to go to a place which he was to receive as an inheritance; and he went out, not knowing where he was to go' (Heb 18:8).

The Promise

'And I will make you a great nation' (Gen 12:2). The word is *goy* ('nation') and not *am* ('people'); *goy* is a political term and requires a territorial base. Abraham came into the land of Canaan. And there at last he was told of the goal—a telling that was word of promise. 'Then the Lord appeared to Abram and said, "To your descendants I will give this land"' (12:7). In the primitive covenant ritual of Genesis 15 it is made abundantly clear that the land is gift and is received as such. True enough,

Abraham makes preparations (15:9-11), but at the divine bidding, and Yahweh alone performs the rite (v.17). Abraham had been smitten with the *tardemah,* a divinely provoked sleep (v.12). As thoroughly as the Man who was to receive his helpmate (2:21), Abraham is 'out cold'. Yahweh alone is awake and active: the land is gift as fully as the Woman was gift. The covenant rests on God's initiative and unconditional promise and asks only for trust. Twice more will Abraham hear the word of promise (17:8; 24:7) and promise it will remain for him and his descendants for generations to come. Yet, Abraham will take steps to win himself a title to this land. The cave of Machpelah, a burial place for Sarah, which he insisted on *purchasing* from the Hittites (23:4-20), gives him a foothold in *his* land. But he remains a sojourner.

The promise of the land is rooted in paradox. The beginning of salvation history sees a landed man called from city and homeland and launched into a situation of landlessness. The one who receives the promise of the land will himself, henceforth, live as a landless wanderer. He is sustained by that promise alone. And so it will be for his successors.

In Genesis the story of Abraham (12:1-25:18) and the story of Jacob form two contrasting blocks. Isaac is found in both cycles as but a pale figure: son of Abraham and father of Jacob and little more than that. The 'family' of Abraham, Isaac and Jacob veils a complex situation: the grouping of the elements that went into the shaping of the 'people of Yahweh'. Folk-memory had preserved recollections of ancestral tribes—an 'Abraham' tribe, an 'Isaac' tribe, a 'Jacob' tribe, and others to some extent present in the 'twelve sons' of Jacob. The familiar genealogy expresses a people's awareness of its identity. In the stories as we have them, Abraham and Jacob, taken as individuals, are painted in vivid colours.

Faith, Tried and True

From the start, Abraham is the man of faith. Yahweh is fully aware of the difficulty of what he asks: Abraham must leave everything. Later, despite the advanced age of Abraham and Sarah and her barrenness, Abraham puts his faith in Yahweh, confident that he will be ancestor of numberless descendants (15:5-6). And then there is the 'sacrifice' of Abraham, his readiness to sacrifice the child of promise: Isaac (22:1-19). A poignant story indeed. 'Take your son, your only son Isaac whom you love... and offer him as a burnt offering.... So Abraham rose early in the morning'. The man who had, without hesitation, at the Lord's bidding set out from his homeland, now, without question, sets out to do this awful deed. He obeyed with a heavy heart, a heart pierced to the quick by Isaac's unsuspecting question: 'My father, behold the fire and the wood; but where is the lamb for a burnt offering?' Likely, behind this narrative or within it, is a polemic against human sacrifice—something always abhorrent to Yahwism. But the tragic dignity of Abraham and his sad readiness to give his son stirred a Christian sentiment. The deed of Abraham has surely coloured the telling of a greater love: 'He who did not spare his own Son but gave him up for us all' (Rom 8:32); 'God so loved the world that he gave his only Son' (Jn 3:16). Abraham had put his faith in God, a seemingly capricious and callous God. For, Abraham saw, what Paul and John were to recognise, that his God is always a foolish God—a God who loves with divine abandon. He can make outrageous demands because he will always be faithful.

After all this it is encouraging to discover that Abraham has his weak side. He is prepared to jeopardise Sarah to save his own skin—'she is my sister' (12:10-20). Later, he worked out to his own satisfaction how the promise might be fulfilled—through the surrogate motherhood of Hagar (Ch.16). And when he first heard the promise of the birth of Isaac he reacted with amused incredulity (17:15-16). Still, the verdict of Paul stands: Abraham is man of faith (Gal 3:6-9); Rom 4:1-3).

JACOB AND REBEKAH—*Con-man and his Mother*

With Jacob we are in another world. The Jacob-stories (Gen 25:19-35:29) are laced with humour—sometimes black humour. Jacob is not an attractive character. He is the archetypical con-man. From the start his astuteness is signalled: born second of a pair of twins, he came forth from the womb with a firm grip on Esau's heel (25:26). It will come as no surprise, then, to find that later he will trick poor Esau out of his birthright—his right of primogeniture, of firstborn (25:29-34). Jacob had a capable ally in his mother Rebekah—he is her white-haired boy. A blind Isaac sensed the approach of death and craved one good dinner before the end. He asked Esau (his favourite) to hunt down game and cook it for him. Rebekah had taken care to overhear the request and determined to turn it to her darling's advantage. The subterfuge of covering the smooth hands and neck of Jacob with goat-skins so that he might pass for the hairy Esau certainly calls for a 'suspension of disbelief'! But the trick worked and Jacob received the blessing of the firstborn. Esau and Isaac had been outwitted (27:1-40). It might seem to us that Isaac, when he had become aware of the deception, could simply have altered his will, to put it like that. The point of the story is that a blessing once bestowed could not be withdrawn. Rebekah had played on that and had won. As well, she resolutely overcame Jacob's fear. He had no scruple about pulling the wool over the eyes of his senile father, but he feared an outraged father's curse. His mother had no hesitation: 'Upon me be your curse, my son; only obey my word' (27:13). Thus reassured, Jacob was eager to comply. And so it was that Jacob became ancestor of the Twelve Tribes of Israel.

The story continues in a similar vein. Jacob judged it a prudent move to get out of range of an understandably peeved Esau and went off to his uncle Laban in Haran. Trickery ran in the family and we have a battle of wits between uncle and nephew. The rascally Laban proved a more formidable opponent than the feckless father and brother. Even then, though he lost a battle or two, Jacob won the war. And, yet again, he was able to out-manoeuvre his brother Esau (32:3-33:17). Altogether, not a savoury character—yet, he was furthering God's purpose.

Wrestling with God

He had his good points, though. There is his prayer (32:9-12) as he fearfully prepared to meet his brother. He protested: 'O Lord...I am not worthy of the least of all the steadfast love and all the faithfulness which you have shown to your servant' (v.10). Earlier, on his way to Haran, he had his dream at Bethel—the dream of Jacob's ladder: 'He dreamed that there was a ladder set up on the earth, and the top of it reached to heaven; and behold, the angels of God were ascending and descending on it!" (28:12). It is a meeting place of God and humankind. The image is caught up by the Johannine Jesus: 'Truly, truly, I say to you, you will see heaven opened, and the angels of God ascending and descending upon the Son of man' (Jn 1:51). Then there is the strange episode of Jacob's wrestling-bout with God (Gen 32:24-32) when he is told: 'you have striven with God and with men, and have prevailed' (v.28). A Jacob who had adeptly dealt with men (Esau, Isaac, Laban) had successfully contended with God. He had come to see that a genuine relationship with God could not be a merely passive one; it entailed personal effort, striving, a wrestling with the divine will. Jacob had matured, had grown in wisdom.

'Now the die has been cast: The old Jacob, Jacob the trickster, the Jacob who measured life against his own requirements, his own power and his own success—always at the cost of other people, even at God's cost—this Jacob no longer exists. His encounter with God has transformed him. He emerges from it a new person, a person who has at long last come to himself, even if only under compulsion. Now he has been blessed—and also wounded: when the night is past, Jacob is lame in one hip. From a struggle like this, when a person is confronted by his God, no one ends up as he began. But the pain of this newly created Israel ["You shall no longer be Jacob but Israel, for you have entered into a struggle with God", 32:28] recedes in the face of the new experience: "The sun rose upon him" (32:31). Now the world and his own life—and his God—all look different: "So Jacob called the name of the place

Peniel, saying, 'For I have seen God face to face, and my life was preserved'" (32:30). Now he has learnt *how* this God saves, and *whom* he saves: *he saves through conversion and renewal.*[3]

Vehicle of Promise

What matters most is that, from the first, though he seemed unpromising material, Jacob was vehicle of the divine promise. Though he had stolen his father's blessing, it was blessing, and was repeated as Isaac sent him off to Laban (28:3-5). In his Bethel dream he heard the assurance: 'the land on which you lie I will give to you and your descendants; and your descendants shall be like the dust of the earth, and you shall spread abroad to the west and to the east and to the north and to the south; and by you and your descendants shall all the families of the earth bless themselves' (28:13-14). Later, again at Bethel, the promise was repeated (35:9-13). Finally, before his departure for Egypt to find a home with Joseph he was comforted at Beersheba:

> I am God, the God of your father; do not be afraid to go down to Egypt; for I will there make of you a great nation. I will go down with you to Egypt, and I will also bring you up again; (46:3-4)

Jacob's native cunning would have availed him nothing if his God had not been with him.

Jacob raises the question: where is God to be found? The Jacob story carries the consoling message that God is even in the grey areas of human connivance and self-interest. The Jacob story tells us that God takes us as we are. He smiles at our 'wisdom' because our wisdom can serve his folly. Jacob lived by his wits, manipulated people, was a successful 'operator'. The irony of his story is that, in a strange way, he did measure up to his role and status. This was most poignant in his grief for his lost son (Joseph) and for the sons he feared would be lost (Simeon, Benjamin) [37:34-5; 42:36]. In spite of his earthiness he can still mirror something of a God 'who did not spare his own Son'—a God who grieved over the murder of his Son. If Jacob served God's purpose he was no human pawn. His grief is his redeeming feature because it joined him with a caring, grieving God.

MOSES—*Leader*

The land of Goshen, where Jacob and his sons found a home (Gen 47:1-6, 27-8) could never be their abiding home. It was in the desert that Israel would learn to know Yahweh. When they had come into the land of promise and had succumbed to its temptation, a prophet could look back to the brief honeymoon of God and his people: 'Therefore, behold, I will allure her, and bring her into the wilderness, and speak tenderly to her.... And there she shall answer as in the days of her youth, as at the time when she came out of the land of Egypt' (Hos 2:14-15).

Moses fled Egypt with a motley crowd of slaves. In the desert, at Sinai, they became the people of God (Ex 19:1-Num 10:28). The covenant formula—'I will take you as my people and I will be your God'—does not point to a pact between equals. God gives the covenant. His people commit themselves and undertake to serve Yahweh and live by his commandments. If, in the tradition of Israel, Abraham is father of the people, Moses is architect of the nation. His role in the Exodus story is paramount. It is made abundantly clear, though, that always the supreme actor is the God of Moses. To Moses the name of Yahweh was revealed and it was he who organised the cult. But, just as he is leader of the people of *Yahweh,* he is minister, not founder of the religion of Yahweh.

The descendants of a Jacob who had been warmly welcomed in Egypt were to fall on hard times: 'There arose a new king over Egypt, who did not know Joseph' (Ex 1:8). There was oppression: 'And the people of Israel groaned under their bondage, and cried out for help, and their cry under bondage came up to God. And God heard their groaning' (Ex 2:23-24). God would deliver from bondage and the instrument of deliverance (a 'vessel of election', cf. Acts 9:15) was at hand. Moses, saved from the waters, brought up as an Egyptian, remained an Israelite at heart. In Midian, his land of refuge, God, in the episode of the burning bush, revealed his name: Yahweh (Ex 3:13-15). Whatever the precise meaning of the mysterious name (still disputed by scholars) it is surely meant to match the solemn assurance of v.12: 'I will be with you'. The new name enshrines God's pledge to be efficaciously with his people.

21

Reluctant Liberator

Moses showed himself to be a reluctant liberator. He was evidently shocked by the declaration: 'Come, I will send you to Pharaoh that you may bring forth my people, the children of Israel, out of Egypt' (3:10). Admittedly, it was a daunting prospect for one who had fled Egypt for his life. He came up with a series of objections and excuses: who was he to be sent on such a mission to Pharaoh? The people will want to know the name of this God. In any case, the people will not believe Moses. He is not eloquent and has no hope of getting the message across. Finally, please, please, send someone else! (3:11-4:13). A Lord who had responded graciously to protest after protest ran out of patience: 'Then the anger of the Lord was kindled against Moses' (4:14). Moses got the message. With Aaron as his spokesman he promptly set out on his mission.

The nine plagues (7:8-10:29) witness to a tug-of-war between Moses and Pharaoh. The latter was being given every chance, to no avail. His intransigence will not foil Yahweh's purpose: 'Yet one plague more I will bring upon Pharaoh and upon Egypt; afterwards he will let you go hence; when he lets you go, he will drive you away completely' (11:1). A study of the exodus narrative (12:29-14:31) reveals two distinct episodes involving two groups: an exodus-flight and an exodus-expulsion, and the situation may have been more involved. It is likely enough that Moses was leader of a group which had managed to escape from a pharaonic forced-labour camp and had fled Egypt.

The historical 'exodus' was a petty affair. What really took place is lost forever within the core of a great religious saga. What matters is that the faith of Israel had discerned in Yahweh's concern for oppressed slaves the true character of a God of salvation. The Exodus-saga reflects a long and chequered dialogue between God and people. The stature of Moses grew in tandem with the story. But there had to be a historical Moses as there had to be a historical happening. And, today, enlightened by insights of liberation theology, we can observe that the exodus event—and this remains true even in the saga—was, first and last, a social and political event. Slaves were set free from slavery, delivered from a 'house of bondage' and, eventually, led to a homeland. Significantly, the poet Second Isaiah, in his stirring-up of some enthusiasm for a return from Babylonian exile, casts the return to freedom as a new Exodus (Is 40:3-11). The archetypical redemptive event was, essentially, a liberation. It is a salutary reminder that our God is not in the business of saving 'souls'; he wants to set *people* free. Salvation has to do with humanness, every aspect of true humanness.

Leader and Mediator

Moses was leader and mediator. He was very conscious of his role of intercessor, his service to his people. In that task he was outspoken and generous. He had been sent to free the people. Yet, his approach to Pharaoh seemed only to aggravate their plight. He complains, exasperatedly: 'You have not delivered your people at all!' (Ex 5:23). The same Moses is prepared to put his neck on the block. If Yahweh will not forgive the people's infidelity in the episode of the golden calf, then: 'blot me, I pray you, out of your book which you have written' (32:32). Moses reminds his God that the perverse crowd left in his charge is *God's* people—and *he* might try looking after them for a change! (33:12-13). He is thoroughly fed-up with playing nursemaid to *God's* people (Num 11:11-15). When Yahweh calls his bluff, Moses promptly pulls in his horns. God proposes to destroy the rebellious people and make Moses the father of his new people—but Moses will have none of it (14:13-19). Like a later Jeremiah, while he huffs and puffs, Moses gets on with the job.

One might have expected that Moses, who had so faithfully guided God's people and had suffered so in the process, would have led them, at last, into the Promised Land. And Moses, in understandably human fashion, yearned for just that privilege. He pleads:

> O Lord God, you have only begun to show your servant your greatness and your mighty hand; for what god is there in heaven or on earth who can do such works and mighty acts as yours? Let me go over, I pray, and see the good land beyond the Jordan, that goodly hill country and Lebanon (Dt 3:24-5).

But it was not to be. Moses, the faithful servant, was not to set foot in the land (3:23-29). We cry 'foul' and become indignant. That is because we *will* insist on holding a human scale against God's ways. We must, willy-nilly, accept that his ways will never fit our measure. Why did God treat Moses so shabbily—as we imagine it? In answer to our scruple stands the verdict of Deuteronomy:

> And there has not arisen a prophet since in Israel like Moses, whom the Lord knew face to face (34:1).

The People of Israel

Moses had led the people to the borders of Canaan; it was left to Joshua to bring them into the land (Jos 1:2-3). More significant than the idealised picture of Jos 10-11 (which casts back into the age of Joshua the conquest of David) is the account of the Shechem assembly (Jos 24). If the neat genealogy of the patriarchs offers a stylised version of Israel's origins, the Shechem covenant covers a vital stage of its development. Those who had come to Canaan from Egypt would have found groups who had never been in Egypt. Some of these were willing to acknowledge the God, Yahweh, of the Moses-group. The Shechem assembly marks this amalgamation. While our account of the Shechem covenant is overlaid with deuteronomic theology, it is not a creation of the deuteronomists but is far older. At Shechem 'all the tribes of Israel' made solemn declaration: 'We will serve Yahweh, for he is our God' (Jos 24:18, 24). 'So Joshua made a covenant with the people that day, and made statutes and ordinances with them at Shechem' (24:25). The 'people of Yahweh' of Moses had grown into the people of Israel.

Pilgrimage

Moses had led the first pilgrimage of the people of God: a journey from slavery to freedom. In biblical tradition, Egypt would recur as symbol of oppression and bondage. The land of Palestine would function as a promise fulfilled. Even when the land was lost, it would again emerge as promise of restoration. The pilgrimage was a rough passage and not only because of desert hardships and hostile harassment. The deeper journey was a troubled pilgrimage of faith. Throughout Exodus, more markedly in Numbers, there is a struggle between God and people with Moses in the heart of the maelstrom. He did not emerge unscathed (Num 20:12). Yet, it was he who put his finger—in a challenge to his God—on the abiding characteristic of the God of the Bible, the goal of pilgrimage:

> Pardon the iniquity of this people, I pray you, according to the greatness of your steadfast love, and according as you have forgiven this people from Egypt even until now (Num 14:19).

If our God is not a God of steadfast love—he is not God.

JEPHTHAH—*Tragic Warrior*

The account of the conquest of Canaan as presented in Joshua is complex. There is enough evidence to show that, at the death of Joshua, the Promised Land was still far from being conquered. The Israelites, for the most part, held only the hill regions and were quite unable to dislodge the better armed Canaanites from the plains. They had to wait two centuries before the whole land was theirs. What the deuteronomical editors of the story did was—notably in chapters 10 and 11—to superimpose a simplified and idealised picture of the conquest. In its turn, the Book of Judges bears the unmistakable deuteronomic stamp. The main part of the book (Jg 3:7-16:31) is a compilation of disparate traditions concerning various 'Judges'—local charismatic heroes. These traditions are presented from a definite and clearly-expressed viewpoint, a point of view that is set out in the original introduction to the work (2:6-3:6). It is repeated further on (10:6-16) and is also indicated in the formulas which recur at the beginning of the account of each of the 'greater' Judges. The viewpoint is this: The Israelites have been unfaithful to Yahweh; he has delivered them to oppressors; the Israelites have repented and have called on Yahweh; he has sent them a saviour, the Judge. This is a cycle of infidelity, punishment, repentance and deliverance.

25

A prime concern of the deuteronomic editors of the history Joshua to Kings is to give a theological explanation of the catastrophe of the Babylonian conquest and exile: it was occasioned by the unfaithfulness of the people. A more earnest concern was to point a way out of the impasse. The twofold lesson is cleverly made in Judges. For, when trial and oppression have ceased, after a short period of tranquillity, the infidelities recommence and the cycle beings all over again. The lesson is clear. The chastisement of the Exile is not at all unprecedented (except in scale). The story of the ancestors shows a God never tiring of rescue and deliverance. There is a condition though: conversion. The people of the Exile are being reminded that they stand at the second stage. If they will but earnestly come back to the Lord then restoration will surely follow. This theological framework is all that links the diverse stories. We may look to two of the 'heroes': Jephthah and Samson.

Jephthah

The Transjordan tribes of Gad and Reuben were in difficulties. they were under pressure from the Ammonites, and the Palestinian tribes, in conflict with the Philistines, were unable to help. The situation was desperate. Then it was that Jephthah came into his own. Jephthah was born illegitimate and when his legitimate brothers came of age, they kicked him out. He was, evidently, resourceful and became leader of a brigand band. When his people of the tribe of Gad found themselves at the mercy of the Ammonites they turned, in desperation, to the only one of them who had any military experience, one who had some leadership qualities. Jepthah relished the situation and was not reluctant to point out that he was fully aware that they had turned to him only because they were stuck. He exploited the situation. He would come to their aid on condition that he would remain their leader when the campaign was over. They had no choice and accepted his terms.

Jephthah promptly displayed leadership talent. To gain time he entered into negotiations with the Ammonities—and used the time gained to build up an army. When he was ready he attacked and defeated the Ammonites. Jephthah was a man of rude faith. He was clear that the battle would be decisive one way or the other. In his religious view an extraordinary gesture was in order. Nothing less than human sacrifice in fact. He made his bargain with God: 'If you will give the Ammonities into my hand, then whoever comes forth from the doors of my house to meet me, when I return victorious from the Ammonites, shall be the Lord's, and I will offer him up for a burnt offering' (11:30-31). He had designated a victim.

Tragedy

Then the tragedy. Jephthah had acted, in good faith, according to his lights. He did defeat the Ammonites and returned, with his troops, in triumph. According to custom, the women came out, with song and dance, to greet the victors. To Jephthah's horror the band was led by his daughter—his only child! Distraught, he told her of his vow. She understood and agreed with him that there was no way out: he 'had opened his mouth to the Lord'. His vow was sacred and must be fulfilled (11:34-36). The girl was young and unmarried. She would never be a mother and must carry to the grave the disgrace of childlessness. She asked only for a stay of two months to mourn this misfortune. Afterwards, she returned home and her father offered her in sacrifice as he had vowed (11:37-9).

One feels for Jephthah. Life had not been easy for him. Indeed he had started off with the deck stacked against him. Despite his violent life-style as highwayman he could display tenderness towards his only child and his love was recip-rocated: the storyteller has movingly conveyed as much in the exchange between father and daughter. For Jephthah victory had become hollow and the coveted role of leader a burden. The light of his life had gone out. The ultimate tragedy of Jephthah—and of his daughter who shared his religious outlook—was that his awful deed sprang from a wrong under-standing of God. His Lord was one whose favour might be won by human sacrifice. Unhappily, the history of religion shows that terrible deeds have been done in the name of religion—all the more terrible when, as with Jephthah, they are wrought in good faith. A false spirituality must follow a warped notion of God. Jephthah had followed his God in his way. His God cannot be our God, nor can his way be our way.

SAMSON—a *Thady Quill*

I have remarked that the stories in Judges are varied; they can be as different as that of Deborah and Barak (Jg 4-5), based on a historical encounter between Israelites and Canaanites, and the rambunctious folk-tale of Samson (Jg 13-16), but the pattern remains the same. While respecting the editorial intent, we should enjoy Samson for the earthy story it is. The editors did evidently appreciate it because, framework apart, they have presented it untouched.

Cork folklore has thrown up a folk-hero: 'the bold Thady Quill'. There does seem to have been a person of that name, but the ballad of Thady Quill is sardonic, with a non-hero cast in heroic guise. At any rate, the resultant 'Thady' is a parish hero, credited with stalwart exploits in the sportsfield and a dashing way with the ladies. While his exploits are military rather than sporting, Samson is very much a Thady Quill character.

The Amorous Hero

Samson, a child of promise, was a 'nazir'—the sign of his dedication to God being his long hair which must never be cut (13:1-14). Endowed with immense strength, he carried on a one-man war against the Philistines. A recognisable story-feature is that of the invincible warrior vulnerable to every pretty face and figure. Samson's romantic encounters carry the story. On his way to the Philistine town of Timnah to visit his future wife, he killed a lion with his bare hands. A swarm of bees nesting in the vulture-picked skeleton provided the stuff of a riddle for his wedding-guests:

> Out of the eater came something to eat;
> out of the strong came something sweet (14:4).

Failure to solve the riddle would cost the guests dear. The answer was prised from him by his wife (v.18), a presage of future disaster.

Samson's exploits against the Philistines lose nothing in the telling. Not content with just setting a match to the harvest-dry standing grain of the enemy, our hero first caught three hundred foxes and used them as his arsonists—with flaming torches attached to the tied-together tails of each pair (15:1-15). Another time he slew a thousand Philistines, with the jawbone of a donkey as his only weapon. His enemies thought they had Samson in their grasp when, with characteristic bravado, he visited the Philistine town of Gaza and found hospitality in the house of a prostitute. Samson, aware of danger, left at midnight. Barred and bolted city gates proved no obstacle to his enormous strength: he simply tore up gate and gate-posts. That feat would have satisfied an 'average' strongman. But not our Samson! he loaded gates and posts on his broad shoulders and dumped them on a hilltop forty miles away. That showed the men of Gaza! (16:1-3).

Then he met Delilah. She wormed from him his secret: the source of his strength lay in the uncut seven locks of his hair—and a blinded Samson ground corn in a prison mill at Gaza (16:4-22). His shorn locks grew again and his strength flowed back. In the temple of Dagon he wreaked his vengeance. 'So the dead whom he slew at his death were more than those whom he had slain during his life' (16:30). A brilliant ending. To savour this clever narrative, one must take the episodes of the foxes and city gates in one's stride, must not ask why Samson, in the light of his previous experience, would have yielded to Delilah's blandishments, nor wonder why the Philistines could have overlooked the fact that his hair was growing again.... One does not put such questions to *story*.

And the story is an earthy and humorous one. It may serve to remind us that religion need not be humourless. After reading the Samson story one may intone, as elsewhere: 'This is the word of the Lord.' For, our God has a sense of humour. Otherwise how could he have borne and continue to put up with his exasperating children? Compassion is not enough. We must be prepared to laugh, laugh at the foibles of others, laugh with others and laugh at ourselves. Cheerlessness will lead to depression or to fanaticism. Cheerlessness is not a feature of authentic religion.

RUTH—*the Faithful*

The Book of Ruth, one of the shortest of the Old Testament writings, takes its name from the Moabitess whose story it relates. The date of the writing is uncertain; it might well, in substance, be pre-exilic. It is true, of course, that it found its place in the post-exilic collection of five festal *megilloth* ('scrolls') and was read at the feast of Pentecost. The fact that it presents Ruth as great-grandmother of David (Ruth 4:17) was, undoubtedly, a factor in its survival. In literary form it is close to the modern novel. The author, skilfully and with charm, presents an idyll of simple family devotion and of country life. We see that virtues of generosity and piety are rewarded and we discern the guiding hand of divine Providence over all.

The author (or editor) cleverly exploited the ancestry of David to make a point that had special relevance for the postexilic Jewish community. In the tiny Jewish state the struggle to preserve national identity was a painful one. Some came to regard mixed marriages as a mortal danger to the continued existence of the people of God (Ezra 9-10). An excessively nationalistic and exclusive outlook tended to develop. The editor of Ruth (like the author of Jonah) struck a blow on behalf of a more liberal and universalist outlook. Ruth the Moabitess (a foreigner) had accepted Yahweh as her God (Ruth 1:16) and had entered so wholeheartedly into the Jewish way of life that she is lauded by Boaz for her earnestness in seeking the one kind of marriage that would perpetuate the family name (3:10). Her attachment to Naomi is beautifully touching. The divine favour had come upon her. She became an ancestress of David, a link in the messianic line, as Matthew discerned (Mt 1:5).

The Matchmaker

To turn to the story. 'In the days when the judges ruled' (Ruth 1:1), under pressure of famine, a Bethlehemite, Elimelech, took his wife Naomi and their two sons across the Jordan to Moab. Elimelech died shortly. The young men, who had taken Moabite wives, were dead within ten years. Naomi decided to return to Judah and advised her daughters-in-law to remain in their homeland. Ophrah agreed, but the other, Ruth, refused to leave her mother-in-law:

> Entreat me not to leave you or to return from following you; for where you go I will go, and where you lodge I will lodge; your people shall be my people, and your God my God (1:16).

The two women reached Behelehem at barley harvest. Ruth went to glean and, by chance, started in a field owned by Boaz, kinsman of her late husband. Boaz had heard of the devoted young foreigner who had not abandoned her mother-in-law and he treated her with marked generosity (2:1-18). Naomi, intrigued, discerned the hand of Providence. She decided to give Yahweh a helping-hand. Threshing time came, with its celebrations. Naomi had counselled Ruth to seek out a Boaz sleeping near the threshing-floor and lie down at his feet. On waking during the night, he was startled to find a woman at his feet. She told him who she was and then went on to plead: 'Spread the skirt of your robe over your servant' (3:9). In effect, she was asking him to marry her (Dt 23:1; Ezek 16:8). Boaz, who had grown in admiration of the young woman during the days of reaping, also recognised that she was intent on fulfilling an obligation to her late husband. She was seeking to implement the custom of levirate (cf. Dt 25:5-10) which required that a brother or nearest male relative of a childless widow should marry her and father a posthumous descendant for the deceased. (Where Sheol was the end, one might find 'immortality' in one's descendants). There was, too, the question of 'redeeming' the property of Elimelech, of ensuring that it remained in the family. Boaz was suitably impressed by the determined *pietas* of this remarkable woman. There was one snag: a closer kinsman than he. It is evident enough, though, that Boaz will manage to dispose of the obstacle (Ch. 3).

Boaz encountered the claimant at the town gate; in effect, he summoned him to court (4:1-12). Astutely, he raised only the sale of Elimelech's property; the man, who had first option, was quite happy to buy it. Only then did Boaz intimate that the widow of Elimelech's late son was part of the deal. The next of kin, recognising that he might lose out in the affair, renounced

31

his claim. Whereupon, Boaz married Ruth. Before long the afflicted Naomi (1:21) rejoiced in a grandson, whom she adopted (4:16). 'They named him Obed; he was the father of Jesse, the father of David' (4:17).

Throughout, Boaz figures as a thoroughly decent man. There is more than a suggestion that he was adroitly manipulated by the women. But all turned out well. Ruth is a touching human story. There is, in the relationship of Naomi and Ruth, an edifying love-bond between mother-in-law and daughter-in-law. There is the charming touch to the wiles of women: two admirable women who do, gently, manipulate an admirable man. There is the message that romance, and a dash of female wiles, are precious human values. We should be grateful that we have the gift of the Song of Songs, that celebration of sexual love. It was after his creation of man and woman and his blessing on their union that the Creator-God looked benevolently on 'everything he had made, and, behold, it was very good'. (Gen 1:31).

DAVID—*Flawed Saint*

Pressed by Canaanites and, more dangerously, by Philistines (newcomers like themselves) the 'tribes', the groups that had gone into the shaping of Israel, lacking centralised government, stood in mortal danger. The model of monarchy was to hand in the neighbouring Semitic statelets. The monarchist tradition (1 Sam 9; 10:1-16; 11) acknowledges that a like development was inevitable if the nation was to survive. Moreover, it was the will of Yahweh, disclosed to Samuel (9:16). But there was another trend, vehemently opposed to kingship (1 Sam 8; 10:17-25; 12) of which Samuel is also spokesman (8:7). It is evident that as history of the institution, the accounts are incompatible. What they do represent is two theological traditions standing in tension. Each is true in its measure. A theology, simply because it is a human construct, can never be the whole truth.

Whatever reservations there may have been in some

quarters, the idea of kingship was readily accepted. The first venture ended in failure (1 Sam 13-2 Sam 1). The kingship of Saul began in promising fashion, but the first king had too much to contend with, not least his own character. He became a very sick man. Saul is a tragic figure, not without nobility. When Saul had failed, hope was pinned on David—initially by Judah only. A period of civil war represented not opposition to kingship but animosity of north and south. David prevailed, established the united kingdom of Judah and Israel and a modest empire that was to last until the death of Solomon. By that fact, David took his place with Abraham and Moses as an architect of Israel. In his case, too, there is a divine promise:

> The Lord declares that the Lord will make you a house. When your days are fulfilled and you lie down with your fathers, I will raise up your son after you, who shall come forth from your body, and I will establish his kingdom .... And your house and your kingdom shall be made sure for ever in my presence and your throne shall be established for ever (2 Sam 7:11-12, 16).

The Statesman

It could be argued that David is the most fascinating character in the Old Testament. Of course, he has had the inestimable advantage of having had a brilliant biographer. David simply steps, a real-life figure, from the pages of 1,2 Samuel. He is the erstwhile shepherd who slew an enemy champion, and a talented musician who could soothe his troubled king. We learn of David's warm friendship with Jonathan, Saul's son, and of his love for Michal, Saul's daughter (1 Sam 16-2 Sam 1). His days of exile and brigandage ended (1 Sam 16-2 Sam 1)—a paranoid Saul had turned against him—we read in 2 Sam 2-8 of how David came to be king, first of Judah and then of the united kingdom of Judah and Israel. In a shrewd political move he had won for himself the Canaanite stronghold of Jerusalem and made it his capital—the City of David (2 Sam 5). He thus broke free of any special claim of the people of Judah on their Bethlehemite king and mollified the people of Israel, suspicious of undue Judaean influence. Besides, by installing the ark of Yahweh there he turned Jerusalem into the religious centre of his domain. Then, adverting to the incongruity that he had a palace while the ark of Yahweh was still housed in a tent, he planned to build a temple but was informed by the prophet Nathan that the temple was not to be his achievement. The Lord had pre-empted his plan. David had hoped to build a house (temple) for Yahweh; instead it is Yahweh who would build a house (dynasty) for David (7:4-17): 'And your house and your kingdom shall be made sure for ever before me; your throne shall be established for ever' (7:16). In a long and moving prayer (7:18-29) David thanked the Lord for his favour.

The Sinner

Before long we are sharply reminded that David had his weak side. He cast his eye on Bathsheba, wife of one of his officers, and committed adultery with her. It is clear that the affair was an open secret; the husband Uriah was aware that he had been cuckolded (11:1-13). David's next move was wholly unworthy of one who before and again displayed greatness—he engineered the death of Uriah (11:12-25). It was cold-blooded murder. The redeeming feature is that, when challenged by a prophet, David acknowledged his double sin (12:1-15). The prophet obviously expected the confession and repentance of his king—not even the king might flout the law of Yahweh. And it is to David's credit that he saw it so. He made no excuses. The sequel shows him free once again of his disastrous aberration and measuring up to his true stature (12:15-23).

The Bitter Harvest

David had repented, but he had sown his dragon's teeth; he must reap the harvest of bitter family strife. For all his greatness he was flesh and blood and knew his times of frailty and of failure. We have seen something of that weakness. We learn that the gifted statesman who could achieve and maintain the unity of two kingdoms (Judah and Israel) was a disaster as a family man. He indulged his sons to the extent that he would become, not once but twice, target of their ambition. He barely escaped, not replacement but death as well, at the hands of his favourite, the handsome and arrogant Absalom (13:1-19:8). Touching indeed is the king's anguish at the death of this son who had sought his life:

34

And the king was deeply moved, and went up to the chamber over the gate, and wept; and as he went, he said, 'O my son Absalom, my son, my son Absalom! would I had died instead of you, O Absalom, my son, my son!' (18:33).

The story of David ends on a sad note (1 Kings 1). We find him 'old and advanced in years'. He was out of touch and his plans for the succession were very nearly circumvented by another ambitious son, Adonijah. The senile king had to let others bring about what he had decided. The redoubtable Bathsheba, ably supported by the prophet Nathan, thwarted the attempted coup and brought her son Solomon (David's nominee) to the throne. It is, or might be, disturbing to hear David's last commission to the new king (2:5-9). He wanted him to deal with Joab, his veteran friend and army commander, a man who was guilty of two political assassinations. And he instructed him to kill, too, the Shimei who had cursed David as he fled from Absalom (2:5-9; cf. 2 Sam 16:5-12). David was a man of his time. Murder had to be avenged, and Joab was guilty. A curse was efficacious unless turned against its originator.

We take our leave of David the scarred warrior and marred servant of Yahweh. Hamlet's verdict on his father is apposite: 'He was a man, take him for all in all. . . .' At any rate, the lusty and vulnerable David of 2 Samuel is much more congenial than the 'saint' of 1 Chronicles 11-29—a typical piece of hagiography. With all his faults, he remains a hero of God's people. It was he who established Zion as religious centre of Israel. As traditional author of the Psalms he was a framer of Israel's cultic tradition. It was he who heard the promise that his kingdom would not end. It was a promise fulfilled—beyond the expectation and comprehension of David—in the Son of David, the Son of God (cf. Rom 1:3-4).

The Saint

I have named David 'flawed saint'. What saint has not been flawed? Heroic virtue in one age can seem folly in another. Saints, attractive perhaps in their day, may seem repulsive in another time. Not that David might ever look repulsive—he was too honestly human for that. He had faults as well as virtues. The encouraging word of his life is that if one can rise and then fall—one can rise again. David was a man who had the decency to admit his sin, a man who learned from his tragic experience. He was a man who loved not wisely but too well, loved women and his sons. He proclaims that it is better to love unwisely than not to love at all. In his way he mirrored the foolish love of God—and of his Son.

AMOS—*Liberation Theologian*

The Davidic covenant (2 Sam 7:4-16) aimed at incorporating the monarchy into the earlier tradition of the covenants of Shechem (Jos 24) and Sinai (Ex 19-24). The great achievements of David must have convinced many that the promise to the patriarchs had been fulfilled. That achievement included establishing Jerusalem as the religious centre of the nation. A theology grew up about Jerusalem and the Davidic monarchy which would become official in the cult of the Temple. It was believed that Yahweh had chosen Mount Zion as the seat of his earthly rule; he would be the unfailing protector of his people (Ps 48:12-14). And it was believed that he had chosen David as his designated king and had made with him an everlasting covenant that his dynasty would never end (Ps 89:3-4, 19-37).

The covenant with David was understood as a promissory covenant after the pattern of that with Abraham (Gen 15:1-21). No conditions attached to the promise, and though individual kings might fail, the dynasty would be eternal. Zion might be endangered; it could never fall. The existing order of the nation was willed by God and founded by God. Yahweh would dwell forever among his people, would reign on Mt Zion. He would be their shield against their foes and would guarantee the unfailing dynasty of David.

And yet, the historical kingdom of David did not stand. It soon became a divided kingdom. In 721 BC Israel fell to the Assyrians and disappeared from history. In 587 Judah fell to Nebuchadnezzar. This must have seemed the end. The house built by Abraham and Moses and David had crashed in ruins. The promise of Yahweh had failed. Already, in the deuteronomic verdict on the dual disaster, we have the beginning of an answer: 'The Lord was very angry with Israel, and removed them out of his sight' (2 Kgs 17:18). 'And the Lord said, "I will remove Judah also out of my sight, as I have removed Israel, and the temple of which I said: My Name shall be there"' (23:27).

For the land proved to be not only blessing and fulfilment, it was also temptation. Possession brought with it security, self-sufficiency. And because possessions were a concrete sign of blessing, they brought a fatal religious complacency. The prophets inveighed, fruitlessly, against this complacency. It took the Exile and its experience of landlessness to shatter it. Tragically, following on restoration came a new basis of security, a more insidious ground of complacency. People would find comfort in religion rather than in living faith, would find refuge in observance against the risk of decision.

Troublers of Israel

One would expect that the great prophets had something worthwhile to say about the promise and the land. They were, all of them, heirs of Abraham and of Sinai, and some were supporters of the house of David. They lived in troubled times and lifted voices of protest. Casting a cold eye on the past and the present of the nation, they raised the question of its very survival. Could it come under God's judgment and be destroyed? or, must God preserve his people at any price—even in spite of their gross unfaithfulness? What do promised land and chosen people ultimately involve?

The typical Israelite prophet is a man who has received a divine call to be a messenger and interpreter of the word of God. He is one who has met with God. The word which has come to him compels him to speak. 'The Lord has spoken, who can but prophesy?' asks Amos (Am 3:8). Jeremiah, despondent because of his unrelieved message of woe to the people he loved, would stifle the word: 'If I say, "I will not mention him, or speak any more in his name", there is in my heart as it were a burning fire shut up in my bones, and I am weary with holding it in, and I cannot' (Jer 20:9). Not only the words of a prophet but his actions, even his life, are prophecy. The marriage of Hosea is a symbol (Hos 1-3). Isaiah and his children are signs (Is 8:18). Ezekiel multiplies prophetic mimes (Ezek 4:3; 12:6, 11;24:24). Whatever the form of the message, the prophet's vision of God had permeated the manner of his thought so that he saw things from God's point of view and was convinced that he so saw them.

Armed with this conviction, the prophet was outspoken, a merciless critic of the people and of the establishment. Each of the great prophets richly deserved the epithet petulantly branded by Ahab on Elijah: 'troubler of Israel' (1 Kgs 18:17). The prophets were not comfortable people to have around. But the world of Israel, and our world too, is so much the richer because of them.

Amos

Amos is the earliest of the Old Testament prophets whose words have been preserved for us in book form. The heading of the book (Am 1:1) tells us that Amos was a peasant of Tekoa (about six miles south of Bethlehem) and that he was active during the reign of the contemporary kings, Uzziah of Judah and Jeroboam II of Israel. Since his ministry was clearly set in the height of Israel's prosperity, it must have been well into the reign of Jeroboam II (783-743)—a reign which marked the apogee of Israel—in other words, around the year 750 BC.

The passage Am 7:10-15 gives a more detailed picture of Amos' background. He spent part of his time as a shepherd and part as a 'dresser of sycamore figs'—this expression refers to a method of helping the fruit to ripen. The mission in Israel of a prophet from Judah is a striking indication that a common religious tradition spanned the divided kingdoms. When Amaziah, priest of Bethel, warned Amos that he should earn his living in Judah—by accepting fees like the professional prophets (cf. 1 Sam 9-8; 1 Kgs 14:3; 2 Kgs 8:8), Amos replied that he was not a *nabi* of that sort, nor was he one of the 'sons of the prophets': ninth-century prophetic groups. Amos had received a personal call.

Justice

Amos was the great champion of justice, who firmly

defended the moral order established by God and enshrined in the covenant. He castigated the disorders that prevailed in an era of hectic prosperity. To his eyes, the symptoms of social decay were glaring. Wealth, concentrated in the hands of a few, and these the leaders of the people, had corrupted its possessors; oppression of the poor was rife; the richly-endowed national religion, with its elaborate ritual, induced a comfortable, self-righteous atmosphere. The prophet set out to shatter this dangerous complacency.

The book of Amos is a compilation, made by his disciples or in prophetical circles, of oracles and sermons of the prophet spoken in various situations. The oracles are genuine on the whole, but the arrangement is not that of the prophet. As we have it, the passage 1:2-2:16 was not delivered all at once; it is a compilation of oracles spoken on different occasions. Yet—like the Sermon on the Mount—it brings out, powerfully, the power of the speaker and impact of his words. We have people of Israel listening approvingly to threatened punishment of six neighbouring nations: Damascus, Gaza, Tyre, Edom, Ammon and Moab. Then comes the climax, the seventh oracle (the oracle against Judah—2:4-5—is a late insertion), and out of the blue the prophet's thunderbolt strikes Israel! He does not mince his words:

> They sell the righteous for silver, and the needy for a
> pair of shoes;
> they trample the head of the poor into the dust ...
> a man and his father go into the same maiden...
> in the house of their God they drink the wine of those
> who have been fined (2:7-8).

There is injustice and oppression of the poor; the degradation of servant girls obliged to satisfy the sexual needs of master and son; the wine of sacred banquets is paid out of illegal fines. Altogether, an unsavoury picture. The womenfolk are no better; the prophet is scathing:

> Hear this word, you cows of Bashan,
> who are in the mountain of Samaria,
> who oppress the poor, who crush the needy,
> who say to their husbands: 'Bring that we may drink!'
> (4:1).

39

A picture of pampered arrogance.

I Despise Your Feasts

Particularly disturbing for the prophet was the prostitution of religion. He returns to it again and again. We have already adverted to the abuse noted in 2:8. He can be bitingly sarcastic:

> Come to Bethel, and transgress, to Gilgal and multiply transgression; bring your sacrifices every morning, your tithes every three days ... for so you love to do, O people of Israel (4:4-5).

The cult was lavish—all the more because the unwonted prosperity was seen as a seal of divine approval on piety. God is not impressed by hypocrisy:

> I hate, I despise your feasts...
> Take away from me the noise of your songs;
> to the melody of your harps I will not listen (5:21,23).

Elaborate cult is no substitute for a lifestyle that matches one's profession of faith in God. Without orthopraxis, not only orthodoxy but the paraphernalia of worship is empty and pointless. The priority is firmly established:

> Let justice roll down like waters,
> and righteousness like an ever-flowing stream (5:24).

A greater than the prophet would make the same point: 'If you are offering your gift at the altar, and there remember that your brother has something against you, leave your gift there before the altar and go; first be reconciled to your brother, and then come and offer your gift' (Mt 5:23-4).

The Day of the Lord

Israel had been chosen by Yahweh—of that there was no doubt. But with the privilege of that choice goes a corresponding obligation: 'You only have I known of all the families of the earth, therefore I will punish you for all your iniquities' (3:2). Israel has received more, and of her more will be required. Amos perceived that the response was lacking and saw that nothing short of a radical change of life could save Israel (5:4-6, 14-15) and he feared that it would not come. He warned those

40

who looked to the 'Day of the Lord' (envisaged as God's intervention on behalf of his people) that the Day would be darkness and not light (5:18). He saw that the slumbering Assyrian giant would soon waken and destroy Israel (3:9-11). There was only one way to avert the wrath to come: 'Hate evil, and love good, and establish justice in the gate; it may be that the Lord, the God of hosts, will be gracious to the remnant of Joseph' (5:15). Faint hope, indeed, and the prophet cannot see it come to anything. His message is one of unrelieved gloom. The present conclusion (9:8-15) was added by editors who wanted the book to close on a positive note.

Amos did not speak in riddles; his message was uncompromising and unmistakable. We are left in no doubt that this was so for, in a revealing passage, we are shown an indignant Amaziah, priest of the Israelite sanctuary of Bethel, sending this troublesome Judaean interloper packing: he had had the effrontery to speak against king Jeroboam in the king's own sanctuary. But Amos took care to have the last word—a word that could bring no comfort to Amaziah or to his royal master (7:10-17). And the true prophet has a disconcerting propensity to be right.

It is not surprising that Amos is a favourite of theologians of liberation. Indeed, his Israel is uncannily like many a country of Latin America, particularly in the grossly unjust distribution of wealth, in exploited poor, and in the privilege and pomp of official religion. The prophet, in the name of his God, speaks out not only against the situation of his day but against injustice in any age. God is always on the side of the oppressed. And God will not be mocked. Pilgrimage, even towards the right goal, does not necessarily lead to God's rest (cf. Heb 3:7-4:13). The rulers of Israel felt assured that they had reached the Promised Land. The prophet would insist that they inhabited a fool's paradise. Pilgrimage may have taken them to a place and a state. It had not brought them to an understanding of the true God. We are warned that a pilgrim people may be following a false god. Or, leaders may hold before them, or foist on them, a god who is not God.

HOSEA—*Prophet of Love*

Few have been better prepared to grasp and express the love of God for his people than Amos's contemporary, Hosea, a native of Israel. He was a man who had known the pain of love. He had loved and married a woman who proved unfaithful. His love was steadfast and he won her back (Hosea chs 1-3). He had the perception to see in and beyond his personal experience the drama of God's love. So close is the link between experience and revelation that it is chapter 2—the love affair of Yahweh and Israel—which leads to a keener grasp of the prophet's personal tragedy.

This Tremendous Lover

In sorrow, Yahweh had divorced his spouse: 'she is not my wife and I not her husband'. Here, as at Babel where his will to scatter humankind out of his sight (Gen 11:1-9) faltered in his call of Abraham to a new beginning (12:1-3), and as at the Flood when his grim decision: 'I will blot out man whom I created from the face of the ground for I am sorry that I have made them' flows directly into the declaration: 'But Noah found favour in the eyes of the Lord' (6:7-8), God is inconsistent. Ever, God's weak side is his love. Divorced Israel may be: the price of unfaithfulness. In God's eyes she is still his spouse and he will not give her up:

> Therefore, behold, I will allure her, and bring her into the wilderness and speak tenderly to her. . . . And she shall answer as in the days of her youth, as at the time when she came out of the land of Egypt. . . . And I will betroth you to me forever; I will betroth you to me in righteousness and in justice, in steadfast love and in mercy. I will betroth you to me in faithfulness and you shall know the Lord.

The prophet's marriage is described in biographical style (ch. 1) and in autobiographical style (ch. 3). The woman, Gomer, whom Hosea married, seems to have been attracted to the worship of Baal and was to become one of the cult-prostitutes mentioned in 4:13-14. As Isaiah would do (Is 7:3; 8:3) Hosea gave symbolic names to his children (Hos 1:4-9) so that he and they became living signs of God's word to Israel. In chapter three we read that the prophet won back his unfaithful wife. The symbolism of the event is clear enough. Marriage with one who was to be unfaithful signifies that Yahweh is the spouse of a people which worships the Baals—in prophetical language idolatry is 'harlotry'. The corrective seclusion of Gomer (3:3) points to a time of trial before covenant renewal; the names of woe given to the children warn of the chastisement of Israel; the renewed marriage life of Hosea and Gomer promises the restoration of good relations between Yahweh and his people.

Hosea was the first to represent the covenant relation of Yahweh with his people as a marriage. It would have seemed natural that the covenant between God and Israel might have been likened to the marriage contract. In fact it is not the contract aspect that is exploited but rather the love aspect and especially the love of a husband for his wife. Hosea harked back to the wilderness and the entry into the land. He looked to the graciousness of Yahweh and the rank ingratitude of Israel (9:10; 11:1-12; 13:4-6). Doubtless, Hosea idealised the wilderness years and painted them as the honeymoon period of God and his people. What matters is that he did not hesitate to cast Yahweh as the Spouse of Israel. Bold imagery indeed when the Canaanite religion of Baal was the great temptation: the fertility cult of Baal and his consort Astarte. The prophet knew that, despite a risk of confusion, what mattered was to proclaim the love of his God. Theological prudence would not deter him from flaunting his profound conviction. Some might misunderstand—too bad. But those who, like himself, had known the joy and pain of love would see in this long-suffering Spouse their one, true God.

I am God and not Man

Hosea was husband and father, father of two boys and a girl (1:4-9). It would appear that, at first, his family life was happy. Like any young father, he rejoiced greatly at the birth of his first child and was engrossed in his little boy. At least we can deduce as much from his chapter eleven; not less than in his second chapter the vibrant language echoes personal experience. Again what matters is that, as then he did not hesitate to present God as Spouse of his people so, now, he daringly pictures him as doting father of a first-born son.

When Israel was a child, I loved him, and out of Egypt I called my son. . . . It was I who taught Ephraim to walk; I took them up in my arms . . . and I bent down to them and fed them (11:3-4).

This love, too, meets ingratitude. The poem had begun on a sad note: 'The more I called them the more they went from me' (11:2). They deserve to be sent back to Egypt again (v.5); he would leave them where he had found them. And he would—but for his vulnerable love:

How can I give you up, O Ephraim. . . . My heart recoils within me, my compassion grows warm and tender. . . . I will not again destroy Ephraim. For I am God and not man, and I will not come to destroy (11:8-9).

I am God and not man. Taken out of context (as it often is) it might be an assertion of God's transcendence. For Hosea it is a declaration of God's love. Where human love would say 'Enough' God will never set limits. Paradoxically, 'I am God and not man' expresses the 'humanness' of God. It asserts that God is more 'human' than humankind. It is not by chance that the Son of God, come at last to show humans what being human means, will set nothing else than love as the mark of true humanness.

There is a further point. I have followed the generally accepted exegetical course of taking the image of Hosea 11 to reflect the father-love of God. In fact, a strong case can be made, and has been made, for an understanding of the passage as imaging God's mother-love.[4] One may, in the first place, observe that the picking up of an infant and a bending down to feed (11:3-4) is a vivid description of a mother breast-feeding an infant—all the more indeed when the phrase 'lifting to the cheek' may be better rendered 'lifting to the breasts'. More thought-provoking is v. 9: 'I am God and not man'—'man' is not *adam* ('humanity') but *ish*: specifically male. Yahweh is rejecting *male* behaviour for himself. He is not going to act with stern anger and destroy his people; strong maternal emotions resist such conduct on his part. In ch. 11, then, Yahweh as mother is a warm image of God for Hosea. What is undoubted is his stress on God's measureless love.

A Morning Cloud

This divine *hesed* is demanding. There is always need for *metanoia*, for conversion. Repentence must be sincere; the Lord desires integrity. There is no place for facile conversion. Fine words are not enough.

> Come, let us return to the Lord;
> for he has torn, that he may heal us;
> he has stricken, and he will bind us up...
> Let us know, let us press on to know the Lord;
> his going forth is sure as the dawn;
> he will come to us as the showers,
> as the spring rains that water the earth (6:1, 3).

Noble sentiments—but without substance. They voice the approach of those who would presume on Love. Such would flatter the Lord with elaborate cult, with lavish sacrifices. But he is God and not man; he will not be flattered:

> Your love is like a morning cloud,
> like the dew that goes early away (6:4).

A far cry from loving the Lord with all of heart and soul and mind. It will not do:

> For I desire steadfast love and not sacrifice,
> the knowledge of God rather than burnt offerings (6:6).

Religion is not the same as faith and not the same as love. Religion can be the easy way out. It can be salve to an uneasy conscience or down payment on the future. God is not mocked. Love and service are what count. There is no substitute.

Hosea was to speak of judgment too. He warned of the approaching Assryian danger (13:15). It will come like a whirl-wind (6:7) and soon (10:15), bringing destruction (8:14; 12:12) and death (14:1) in its wake. He castigated abuses in Israel (4:1-3), laying the blame at the door of the priesthood (4:4-19) and of Israel's political leaders (5:1-7). Like Amos, he was critical of religion that was show, without substance: 'Because Ephraim has multiplied altars for sinning, they have become to him altars for sinning' (8:11). Fascinating is the stark contrast between 13:12-16 and 14:1-8. In the first passage there is total rejection of Israel; then there is a passionate appeal to conversion, an appeal with a reassuring promise: 'I will heal their faithlessness; I will love them freely, for my anger has turned from them' (14:4). The contrast is a splendid example of the Hebrew penchant for thinking in contrasts without qualification. Similarly, the Hebrew God is not—unlike the Greek God—prisoner of his own divinity. He is disconcertingly free and is not troubled by contradiction. For his abiding characteristic is *hesed*, his faithful goodness. And that has nothing to do with logic. Hosea's last word is, fittingly, a word of hope: 'What has Ephraim to do with idols any more, when I hear him and watch over him? I am like an evergreen cypress, you owe your fruitfulness to me' (14:8).

Two Attitudes

Hosea and Amos illustrate what very different people two prophets might be and how diverse two prophetic messages might sound. Though near contemporaries (Hosea was active later in the reign of Jeroboam II and continued on longer than Amos) and speaking to the same Israel, their message was coloured by their different temperaments—and their different images of God. Amos's message was one of unrelieved gloom. It would seem that his God was a God of justice, a God who went strictly by the book. Israel was unfaithful to the covenant and would persist in unfaithfulness. A just God must and would punish. The God of Hosea was pained by that unfaithfulness—the prophet was very conscious of the guilt of Israel. But, as God of faithful love (*hesed*), he could not let judgment have the last word—'my heart recoils within me'. And Hosea is confident that, ultimately, Love will prevail.

The two attitudes would persist through the religious history of Israel. They are dramatically present in the later contemporary prophets, John and Jesus. The attitudes have run through Christian religious history. If there is a John XXIII there are sure to be prophets of doom. Sadly, there are those who feel duty bound to play Amos. Happier, surely, those who prefer the role of Hosea. They are prepared to take their chance with a God of foolish love.

ISAIAH—*Bionic Prophet*

A first matter that needs taking care of is the complex structure of the book of Isaiah and its broad chronological sweep. The acknowledged scholarly view is that Isaiah falls into three parts: Isaiah 1-39 which contains oracles of the eighth-century prophet, Isaiah ben-Amoz; Isaiah 40-55, known as Second Isaiah; and Isaiah 56-66, often referred to as Third Isaiah. The background of Second Isaiah is the close of the Babylonian captivity, while Third Isaiah is set in Judah in the early days of the return. So far so good. But there is the complicating factor that, in 1-39, only chapter 1-12 and 28-33 give, in the main, the words of Isaiah ben-Amoz—the rest is largely post-exilic. Here, it is enough to advert to this situation, to note that our interest, as regards chs 1-39, is in the authentic words of the eighth-century prophet.

The Words of Isaiah ben-Amoz

'The vision of Isaiah the son of Amoz which he saw concerning Judah and Jerusalem in the days of Uzziah, Jotham, Ahaz and Hezekiah, kings of Judah' (Is 1:1). That title tells us nearly all we know of Isaiah. We can date his mission, in terms of the first and last kings listed, to between 783 and 687 BC. Isaiah, not surprisingly, was rooted in the traditions of Jerusalem and David and firmly believed in the promise made to David. For, in Judah, the promise to David, the Davidic covenant (2 Sam 7), had replaced that of Sinai, and Zion with its temple was the new holy mountain. Hope for the future rested in the Davidic line: 'your house and your kingdom shall be made sure for ever before me; and your throne shall be established for ever' (2 Sam 7:16). The king of Judah was 'son of God' (7:14). The covenant with David was understood as a promissory covenant after the pattern of that with Abraham. No condition attached to the promise; though individual kings might fail, the dynasty would be eternal. The existing order of the nation was willed by God and was founded by God. Yahweh would dwell forever among his people, would reign on Mount Zion. He would be their shield against their foes; no enemy could destroy the holy city and the blessed dynasty. This conviction was the theological basis of Isaiah's hope in the face of seemingly inevitable disaster. Because of it his message was, first and last, trust in Yahweh.

Trust in God. Judah had been prosperous under Uzziah and continued so under Jotham. Like Amos before him, Isaiah attacked luxury and social abuses; this is the burden of many of the oracles of chs 1-5. Yet, his message was, first and last, trust in Yahweh. He could admonish Ahaz when that king, threatened by an anti-Assyrian coalition, would find hope in Assyria. Zion will not fall, nor the Davidic dynasty. But he vainly sought, in Ahaz, the faith that would turn the king from political alliances and enable him to stand, unperturbed, in the face of threats and even in the face of hostile armies. Bluntly he warned him: 'If you will not believe, surely you will not be established' (7:9). Before long that Assyrian help had become a mortal danger. And when Hezekiah, counting on Egyptian help, toyed with the notion of revolt, Isaiah opposed him too, and for the same reason. Despite the weakness and faithlessness of its kings, Zion, in the prophet's eyes, remained inviolable because it was dwelling-place of the Holy God. Sennacherib and his Assyrians would never take the city of David (37:33-5).

Isaiah had lived through the Assyrian threat and knew that catastrophe could indeed strike the nation. But that was because of sin, and it was chastisement, not destruction. Though his experience with kings had led him to lose faith in the historical monarchy, his trust in the promise to the house of David remained firm and his 'messianic' hope found expression in the 'Immanuel' texts, 7:10-17; 9:1-7 and 11:1-9. His ideal king remained a dream and the 'eternal' line of David came to an ignominious end. But the hope was not surrendered. It persisted long beyond the age of Isaiah until the messenger of the Lord would proclaim: 'to you is born this day in the city of David a Saviour who is Christ the Lord' (Lk 2:11).

Immanuel. In Isaiah 7:10-14 Isaiah is vainly counselling his king, Ahaz, at a critical moment when the dynasty of David is in jeopardy (7:1-6). The king's refusal to seek a sign comes not from piety (though he feigns piety) but from the fact that he had already made up his mind to reject the prophet's advice.

One does not so easily dispose of God: Ahaz will have his sign whether he wills or no. Isaiah had taken his stand on God's covenant with David (2 Sam 7). Each successive king of David's line personified the covenant relationship; each was a living reminder and guarantee of the covenant. Ahaz's queen is, at this moment of crisis, pregnant with the one who will continue the threatened line. Isaiah referred to the queen as a 'young woman'; the Greek translation runs: 'a virgin shall conceive' (7:14). Matthew (1:22-3) happily and rightly seized on it to bring out the fact that, although every king of David's line did embody God's promise to be 'with us', only Jesus, son of the Virgin, did it perfectly.

In 9:1-7 Isaiah speaks of a descendant of David and heir to his throne—an ideal king of the future. The passage dates from the dark days when the Assyrian king Tiglath-pileser III had overrun Galilee, the Coastal Plain and Transjordan and turned that territory into three Assyrian provinces: 'the way of the sea, the land beyond the Jordan, Galilee of the Gentiles'. This dynastic oracle pierces the gloom and looks to glorious victory. So confident is the prophet that he speaks in the past tense—all had come to pass. Only at the close, 'the zeal of the Lord of hosts will do this' does he intimate that he is uttering a promise of future salvation. Victory is described in terms of triumph over marauding Midianites in the days of the Judges (cf. Jg 7:1; 8:21). The prince of the future will wear resounding regnal titles. He will rule in justice and in righteousness, and his reign, sustained by God, will endure forever. In the view of Matthew, this prophecy of the coming son of David and of the light to shine on 'Galilee of the Gentiles' was fulfilled in Christ (Mt 4:13-16).

The oracle 11:1-10 is from a later period of Isaiah's ministry. He had been proved right in his assurance to Ahaz that Syria and Israel would not have their way. But the son of the 'young woman' (Hezekiah) had not measured up; he was no 'Immanuel'. The prophet's faith in the divine promise to David remained steadfast as ever but he looked now to a more distant future. He sketches his portrait of the true king. He will be a king Spirit-endowed with the virtues of his ancestors: the wisdom and understanding of Solomon, the prudence and might of David, the knowledge and fear of the Lord of the patriarchs and prophets. Thus endowed, he will rule with 'righteousness'. That is to say, he will champion the destitute and the oppressed. Furthermore, he will restore paradisial peace. The lovely image here has, justly, become proverbial: 'the wolf shall lie down with the lamb . . . and a little child shall lead them'. Prey and predator can feed and sleep in harmony; a child can keep an adder as a pet. All this is metaphor for that future in which distress will be no more and tears will be dried (Rev 7:15-17). It can only come to pass when the earth will be full of 'the knowledge of the Lord'. This is, after all, our Christian hope and our Christian prayer: 'Thy kingdom come, thy will be done on earth . . .'. We must let God be God in *his* way.

Fragile Theology. A century after Isaiah, when Judah was threatened by Babylon, the prophet Jeremiah was to face an impossible task in striving to convince his contemporaries that Nebuchadnezzar, unlike Sennacherib, would have his way and that Zion and its temple would perish. He was not believed. What Yahweh had done in the days of Hezekiah he would surely continue to do. The son of David was son of Yahweh; Zion was city of Yahweh; the temple was his dwelling-place. A young Jeremiah could have adhered to that theology, the comforting theology of a promissory covenant. Always, there was another, and an older, view of God's covenant with his people. Though the Sinai covenant had, at least in Judah, slipped into the background, it had never passed from sight. Here was no unconditional promise. Israel had been given a covenant and had accepted the stipulations of the Lord. It seemed, however, that once in the land, obligations earnestly shouldered in the desert were as readily shrugged off. An older Jeremiah, faced with the patent failure of the Davidic monarchy, looked back to the Sinai covenant. What he was sure of, in the teeth of disaster, was that Yahweh could and would pick up the pieces and put them together again. Yahweh could do what 'all the king's horses and all the king's men' could not do.

For Isaiah the traditional theology could still work. For Jeremiah, not in a very different situation, it no longer made sense. He had to look for another theology, one that really met his situation. Isaiah had looked for an Immanuel, the ideal Davidic king. He would never have recognised that future king in a helpless victim on a cross. One feels that Jeremiah might have met him there. Isaiah (that eighth-century prophet), when put in perspective, alerts one to the fragility of any tidy theological system. God will not be confined. He must be allowed to surprise us. While our faith should grow in firmness, our theology should ever be open, open to the breath of the Spirit, alert to the 'signs of the time'. Today we do not live in the age of Trent. We have witnessed the demise of neo-scholasticism. We must fashion a theology—rather, theologies—for our day.

Second Isaiah

The author of Is 40-55, an anonymous prophet of the Exile, is, for convenience, named Second Isaiah. We have no inkling of the identity of this man, one of the foremost poets and theologians of Israel. All that we do know is that he belonged to the 'Isaian school' and found his inspiration in the work of his eighth-century predecessor. He foretold the end of the Babylonian exile and looked to the Holy One of Israel, the redeemer who would repeat the miracle of the Exodus.

Call to Return. The opening (40:1-11) strikes the note of the Book of Consolation (Is 40-55). The exuberant language serves a purpose. It is evident that, among the exiles, there was little yearning for a return and the prophet has to drum up some enthusiasm. While humanly speaking there were no grounds for optimism, he can assure his people that God is ready once again to bring them out of captivity and into the promised land. This time Yahweh will lead them in solemn procession along a Via Sacra, a processional way hewn through mountain, valley and desert from Babylon to Jerusalem. This time there will be no years of wandering. God will manifest his glory (v.5) through his saving deed on behalf of his people. He is a constant God, unlike the ephemeral grass-like nature of humanity (vv. 6-8). His 'word' stands forever: 'For the mountains may depart and the hills be removed, but my steadfast love will not depart from you' (54:10). Jerusalem is urged not only to welcome her God but to proclaim to the rest of Judah the news of his coming: 'lift up your voice with strength, O Jerusalem, herald of good tidings' (v.9). 'Good tidings': it is here that the New Testament writers found their word 'Gospel', Good News.

The return from the Exile, begun in 536 BC, fell far short of the glowing picture painted by Second Isaiah. Later generations of Jews would have to await in patience the fulfilment of God's word. And the message of restoration might, too, be reinterpreted in moral terms: the highway to be made straight was the path of human life; the kingdom was to be prepared for by repentance. This text and a later understanding of it prepared for the fulfilment that came in the person of Jesus and was ushered in by the Baptist. In the New Testament (following the Greek version of Isaiah) the Baptist has become the 'voice crying in the wilderness' (Mk 1:3).

Cyrus. From the viewpoint of the historian, return from Babylonian exile was a consequence of the military prowess and political astuteness of Cyrus the Persian. But Second Isaiah saw the event in another light. He was convinced, not alone that the meteoric rise of Cyrus had been guided by Yahweh, but that Cyrus had been raised up for one purpose: 'he shall set my exiles free' (45:13). Where Assyria and Babylon had been rods of God's anger against his unfaithful people, Persia will be the instrument of their deliverance. Clearly, the prophet had an accurate perception of the character and policy of the emerging master of the world, but his presentation of a pagan ruler is unprecedented. Cyrus is the 'anointed', the Messiah, of the Lord (45:1) who declares of him: 'He is my shepherd, and he shall fulfil all my prupose' (44:28) and to him: 'I call you by your name, I surname you, though you do not know me' (45:4). Cyrus himself had claimed that he had been called by Marduk (the Babylonian god) to become ruler of the world. Our author firmly counters the claim. He *knows* that Yahweh alone is Lord of history: 'I am the Lord, and there is no other; besides me there is no god... that men may know, from the rising of the sun and from the west, that there is none besides me' (vv. 5-6). The triumph of Cyrus and his benevolent deed on behalf of Israel will demonstrate the Godness of Yahweh. In the setting of Israel's faith this claim, and the prophet's religious reinterpretation of events, made perfect sense. And, seen in this light, the return from the Exile became an expression of Yahweh's unique and universal reign.

The Servant. In Luke's charming story of Jesus and the two disciples on the road to Emmaus (Lk 24:13-35) we have Jesus himself 'interpreting to them in all the scriptures the things concerning himself' (v.27)—precious testimony to a Christian reading of the Old Testament. Just before, he had reminded them that, in God's purpose, the way to glory was the path of suffering (v. 26) a theme found in the Isaian texts known as the 'Servant Songs'. They are: 42:1-7; 49:1-6; 50:4-9 and 52:13-53:12.

In these passages of Second Isaiah the Servant there is a mysterious figure who has been chosen by God and filled with his Spirit (42:1). Though he seems inseparable from the Israel whose name he bears, from the Remnant 'in whom God will be glorified' (49:3), he must lead back Jacob (49:5) and reassemble (49:5-6) and teach (50:4-9) Israel. And he will be the light of nations. Patient (50:6) and humble (53:7) he will, through his suffering and death, accomplish the purpose of God: the salvation of sinners from all nations (53:8, 11-12). The identification of the Servant is a much-debated problem. Nor is it a new question. Already, the minister of an Ethiopian queen, a God-fearer on his way back from pilgrimage to Jerusalem, and reading the text of Isaiah 53, could ask of Philip, one of the seven: 'About whom, pray, does the prophet say this, about himself, or about some one else?' (Acts 8:34).

As likely as not, the Servant may be the prophet himself. What is beyond doubt is that the New Testament writers cast Jesus in the role of the Servant. He, meek and humble of heart, (Mt 11-29) was among his disciples 'as one who serves' (Lk 22:27)—though he was their teacher and Lord (Jn 13:12-15). He had not only given the ultimate proof of his love (13:1; 15:13) but had laid down his life for sinners (Mk 10:45; Mt 20:28). Treated like a common criminal (Lk 23:33) and condemned to death, he was raised up on a cross so that he might draw all to himself (18:31-33); for it was by passing through the suffering and death of the Servant that he entered into the glory of the Son of Man (24:26).

The Two Ways. Deuteronomy proposes a doctrine of the 'two ways': the way of faithfulness to God and his commandments, the way of life; the way of infidelity, the way of death (Dt 30:15-20). In Judges, we have observed, this deuteronomic doctrine is illustrated in terms of a recurring cycle: infidelity—disaster—repentance—deliverance (Jg 2:6-3:6). The deuteronomists offered an explanation of the unparalleled disaster that was the destruction of Jerusalem and the exile. The bottom had fallen out of Judah's world. Yahweh's promises to the patriarchs and to David had gone up in smoke. Was Yahweh a God incapable of protecting and sustaining his people? No; the key to the calamity was the fatal choice of the people: they had walked the way of death. It is not too late. They may still choose life; they may still get back on the right way. Repentance, *metanoia,* will surely lead to deliverance and restoration.

Second Isaiah assumes that those he addressed had learned the deuteronomic lesson. They had come to their senses and had turned back to their God. They are poised for deliverance. He bends his evident poetic talent to the expression of his fervent conviction. There will be, unquestionably, a new Exodus. There will be a fresh flowering. The aftermath would show that the reality did not measure up to his expectation. But there was a change, irreversible. There was a return and a new phase of life for Judah. The enthusiasm he had drummed up was not sustained but he had started something; he had awakened his people to a new understanding of themselves and of their God. His universalist vision was an inspiration and a challenge.

The history of life in Judah in the centuries after the return was to show that, sadly, his vision was lost to sight. The community had found its way but, more and more, that way became *its* way. No longer was there gross infidelity. Instead, fidelity became an obsession. Faithfulness lay in meticulous observance of commandments and statutes, and in ritual. It follows that God could no longer be, truly, a universal God. He could only be the God of those who served him according to the minutiae of Torah.

We are reminded of Vatican II and the post-conciliar Church. The Council, in the celebrated image of John XXIII,

54

was an opening of windows, a letting the wind of the Spirit blow through. It was an opening of minds. For some time now there has been a hardening—there is no doubt of that. There is a certain yearning for a more secure but more closed Church. But there can be no going back.

Third Isaiah

According to the generally accepted view, Isaiah 56-66 is the work of a post-exilic prophet of the Isaian school, and took shape in Palestine some time after the return from the Exile. The author addresses the situation and conditions in the little province of Judah about 520 BC. There had been a return from the exile but the situation was not all that the glowing promise of Second Isaiah might have led one to expect. City and temple are still in ruins; the economic situation is deplorable; there is no organised community; some do not scruple to make a profit out of misery. But, in the midst of this situation the prophet voices the conviction that God's final intervention is at hand.

In Isaiah 56:1-8 the post-exilic prophet makes known the will of Yahweh for his people, the true people of God, that they will open out to embrace even those who are not Israelite at all. In view of the nearness of God's deliverance the people are called upon to observe justice and righteousness. They achieve this not alone by keeping from evil but through religious observance (vv. 1-2). According to Dt 23:1-3 eunuchs and certain foreigners might not enter the assembly of the Lord. Now such are to be made welcome. We meet in vv. 3-7 the universal sweep of Second Isaiah leading to the climactic declaration: 'my house shall be called a house of prayer for all peoples'. Evidently, the second temple is being built (it was dedicated in 515). That temple (no more than Herod's temple was to do) never did welcome all nations. The statement is caught up by Mark in Jesus' words of judgment on the temple (Mk 11:17). In place of it will be built a temple 'not made with hands' (14:58), the temple of his community which will be truly open to all.

Salvation. In 61:1-11 the prophet, speaking in the first person and catching up the words of the first servant Song (Is 42:1), proclaims salvation. His 'anointing' by Yahweh is his missioning: to bring good tidings and proclaim liberation. His mission is to 'the poor', the *anawim,* those whose only recourse is God. In the post-exilic situation such are also economically poor. He takes up and preaches again the message of salvation already urged by Second Isaiah (vv. 1-3). He promises that Jerusalem will be restored. The Jewish people, as a priestly people, will be supported by the labour and wealth of the nations (vv. 4-7); they will be renowned as a people blessed by the Lord (v.9).

The poem closes (vv. 10-11) with the prophet, in the name of Zion, exulting with joy in the good news. Yahweh, whose activity is as sure as the cycle of nature, will clothe Zion in salvation and righteousness. The prophet's exuberance has the same purpose as that of Second Isaiah: in the midst of ruin and devastation, and resultant hopelessness, he holds out glowing promise. Luke tells us that Jesus found in Isaiah 61:1-2 the programme of his own ministry. Coming, one sabbath, to the synagogue of his native Nazareth, he opened the scroll of Isaiah and read out that passage:

> The Spirit of the Lord is upon me,
> because he has anointed me to preach good news to the
> > poor.
> He has sent me to proclaim release to the captives
> and recovering of sight to the blind,
> to set at liberty those who are oppressed,
> to proclaim the acceptable year of the Lord.

Then he declared: 'Today this scripture has been fulfilled in your hearing' (Lk 4:16-21); cf. Is 61:1-2). In this manner a passage, notable in its own right, has been given startling relevance. Jesus made the prophecy his own. He is the Spirit-anointed one who preached good news to the poor. He manifested in his person the tender quality of the promised mercy.

The theme of salvation coming to Zion (Is 61) is continued in chapter 62. The prophet will not cease to utter his message of hope and promise until Yahweh's saving deed shines forth and Zion's mourning is turned to joy. The glory of restored Zion, manifest to the nations, will be God's presence among his people. A new name will reflect a new status. She will be 'My-Delight-in-Her' and 'Married'; no longer 'Forsaken' and

'Desolate'. The marriage image, noted in Second Isaiah (54:1-10) re-emerges. God, the saving and loving bridegroom, will rejoice over a bride whose beauty has been restored. One is reminded of Ephesians 5:25-27—'Christ loved the Church and gave himself up for her . . . that the Church might be presented before him in splendour, without spot or wrinkle or any such thing, that she might be holy and without blemish'.

You are Our Father.   The long poem 63-7-64:17 is a psalm of entreaty written while Jerusalem lay in ruins and the task of rebuilding the temple had not yet begun (cf. 64:10-11). It—especially from 63:15 on—is typical of post-exilic prayers, the 'prayers of the chastened', in that it recalls God's goodness to his people and candidly acknowledges the people's ingratitude and sinfulness. The dominant note, however, is serene confidence in God's loving kindness. The opening statement, 'I will declare the steadfast love of the Lord' (v.7) does not just introduce a chronicle of his mercies of the past; it is assurance that his steadfast love reaches into the present. There is, too, an urgency about the psalm as it strives to bring its hearers to a recognition of their plight from which God alone can deliver them. Not only recognition but acknowledgment: they are expected to make this prayer their earnest prayer.

'Thou art our Father' (63:16; 64-8); the ancestors of Israel, the fathers Abraham and Jacob, lie silent and helpless in Sheol. But Israel is not fatherless. Yahweh is a living, present, and active father: father and redeemer of his people. Because God is one he is cause of everything, cause even of that hardening of heart that led to the disaster of the Exile. This causality remained a mystery to the Israelite; it was never taken to diminish personal responsibility. Here the puzzled and pained question is put in the context of a confident prayer for God's gracious mercy (63:16-17). The prayer continues (64:1-5a) with a plea that God will rend the veil of his heavenly abode and appear in a theophany more majestic than that of Sinai and bring deliverance to his people in distress. A confession of sin follows (vv. 56-7). His people had abandoned their God, to their great loss. Jerusalem, the holy city of his dwelling, lies in ruins. Israel has become an unclean, polluted thing. It has cut itself off from the life-giving sources and has become a heap of withered leaves scattered to the winds. Despite all, indeed *because* of misery and helplessness, there is the comfort that he is Father. Deliverance is readily within the power of the divine Potter as he moulds, to his will, the clay of his people (vv. 8-9). The fact remains, and the challenge is issued: 'Behold, consider, we are all *your* people!' (v.9).

God is not Mocked. Despite the fine words of the prophet the situation on the ground was not bright. Even among the handful of returned exiles division and dissension had emerged. Too quickly, religion became an escape-hatch. Observance would cover a multitude of sins. But God is not fooled: 'They seek me daily and delight to know my ways, as if they were a nation that did righteousness and did not forsake the ordinance of their God' (58:2). It seems that ritual fasting was in vogue—a religious panacea. God is not impressed.

> Is not this the fast that I choose:
> to loose the bonds of wickedness,
> to undo the thongs of the yoke,
> to let the oppressed go free, and to break every yoke?
> Is it not to share your bread with the hungry,
> to bring the homeless poor into your house...
> Then shall your light break forth like the dawn
> and your healing shall spring up speedily (58:6-8).

What God chooses is the 'fast' of justice—he will have nothing less. The irony is that vindication of the poor is 'light and healing', it is liberation—liberation for the oppressor. The oppressor, too, stands in need of liberation, stands in greater need than the oppressed. Few, if any, can find the courage to break free. Liberation of the oppressed is will of God. If it is not of the oppressors' choosing it will come in their despite.

Hope. What does one do when reality does not match up to expectation? One can throw in the towel and bow to the 'inevitable'. But someone has said: 'Better to light a candle than curse the dark.' In the despondency of post-exilic gloom the prophet 'Third Isaiah' dared to hold aloft the torch of his starry-eyed predecessor. True, Second Isaiah seemed to be a romantic visionary. But he could and did cry out: 'I have a

dream!' The dream of Martin Luther King has not wholly
taken shape. But would his people have reached where they are
without his dream? John XXIII, we had thought, had exorcised
the 'prophets of doom'. They are a sturdy breed and are still
with us. Third Isaiah, like Second Isaiah, reminds us of
Christian hope. It has always seemed to me that a pessimistic
Christian is a contradiction in terms. Do we, or do we not,
believe in the promise of our God? The wild exuberance of
those prophets echoes the extravagance of their God. 'Only
God's wild laughter/could hope that things will turn out even'
(Brendan Kennelly).

JEREMIAH—*Sign of Contradiction*

Jeremiah, of all the prophets, is best known to us as an
individual. His book contains many passages of personal confession and autobiography, as well as lengthy sections of
biography. He stands out as a lonely, tragic figure whose
mission seemed to have failed. Yet, that 'failure' was his
triumph as later ages were to acknowledge.

Jeremiah came from Anathoth, a village four miles north-
east of Jerusalem. His father, Hilkiah, was a priest (Jer 1:1).
His prophetic call came in 626 (1:2) while he was still quite a
young man, and his mission reached from Josiah (640-609) to
Zedekiah (597-587) and outlasted the reign of the latter. That
is to say, he lived through the days, full of promise, of the
young reformer king, Josiah, and through the aftermath, the
tragic years that led to the destruction of the nation. It seems
that Jeremiah was initially in sympathy with the aims of the
reform but was disappointed at its eventual outcome. There is
no doubt that he thought highly of the high-minded young
king (22:15-16), but he quickly realised that 'you cannot make
people good by act of parliament'.

What Jeremiah demanded was sincere and heartfelt repentance, an interior change, and what he found was a more
elaborate liturgy which encouraged complacency and invited
hypocrisy (7:21-8; 5:26-31). It was his role to try, in vain, to

bring his people to a genuine change of heart and to hold out hope and lay a foundation for this change, beyond the crucible of national disaster.

The Diary of a Soul

It is possible to trace the spiritual progress of Jeremiah and to see in him the purifying and strengthening effect of suffering, for the most impressive message of the prophet is his own life. He was a man of rare sensitivity with an exceptional capacity for affection—and his mission was 'to pluck up and to break down, to destroy and to overthrow' (1:10) and to cry out, without respite, 'violence and destruction' against the people he loved (20:8). We find in him, to a marked degree, personal involvement (4:19), a feeling of solidarity with the people in their tribulation (8:19-23) and even with the land itself in its devastation (4:23-6). The 'Confessions' are central for an understanding of Jeremiah (11:18-12:6; 15:10-21; 17:12-18; 18:18-23; 20:7-18). They are a record of his communing with his God. Not only are they fascinating because they permit us to gaze into the heart of a prophet; they are encouraging because they let us see how very human the prophet is. Jeremiah had never wanted to be a prophet (1:16; 17:16; 20:7-9) and he continued to discuss the trials of his office with Yahweh throughout his life. He was overwhelmed by the sheer burden, the humanly impossible demand of his task. His prayer is the prayer of Gethsemane.

Baruch, the disciple of Jeremiah, has sketched for us the outward circumstances of the latter's *via dolorosa,* the story of what he had suffered through fidelity to his prophetic vocation between 608 and 587 (Jer 19:2-20:6; 26; 36; 45; 28-9; 51:59-64; 34:8-22; 37-44). He has put his finger on the source of all Jeremiah's suffering. It was the prophet's firm conviction that, at this time, by the instrumentality of Nebuchadnezzar, God was to bring about great changes in the international field, and he would punish Judah with the Babylonian rod of his anger (27:5-11). Consequently, he could hold out no hope of deliverance and asserted, with emphasis, that the capture of Jerusalem was inevitable (37:8,17; 38:3; 34:2). His advice was to surrender without delay (38:17)—advice not welcomed by the war party who had forced the hand of Zedekiah.

The sufferings of the prophet are described with a grim realism that recalls the description of the Passion of Jesus. There are no miracles here, no legion of angels. Jeremiah is abandoned to his enemies and is powerless. And he makes no impression on them. It is not surprising that Christians have seen him as a type of Christ. Jeremiah's clashes with his own prophetical colleagues (those whom we would term the 'false prophets') were probably among his stiffest battles. We can gather this from his tract against the prophets (23:9-40) and from his dramatic encounter with Hananiah (ch. 28). His mission was wholly different from that of his colleagues.

Terror on every Side

No doubt in part as a result of Jerusalem's remarkable deliverance from Sennacherib's army a century before, and on the basis of Isaiah's words, belief in the inviolability of Zion had hardened into a dogma by Jeremiah's time. The notion that the city could fall and the Davidic dynasty end was simply not entertained. The prophets against whom Jeremiah contended were imbued with this outlook (23:32; 28:34, 11). It is understandable that the people listened to their encouraging words rather than to his lonely cry of disaster. Indeed, it appears that he had earned the nickname of old *Magor Missabib* (20:10) from his own familiar warning: 'Terror on every side' (6:25; 20:3; 46:5; 49:29).

His calm conviction that faithless Jerusalem would fall is found, among other places, in his letter to those exiled to Babylon in 598 (29:16-20). Yet, in the same context, he can frame a promise: 'For I know the plans I have for you, says the Lord, plans for welfare and not for evil, to give you a future and a hope' (29:11). This hope is held out not to those left in Jerusalem but to the exiles—a point of view more explicitly expressed in the vision of the two baskets of figs (24:5-7). There is, then, the remarkable factor that the same Jeremiah, who so pitilessly demolished false hope, put before his people a solid hope for the future. His efforts to bring his people to their senses had failed, but it is the greatness of the man, and the grandeur of his faith, that precisely during the most tragic moment of his life he spoke his most optimistic oracles, especially those of chapters 30-33. He saw that the old covenant would be replaced by a new one (31:31-4) when God would touch, directly, the human heart, when he would write his law on the inner self and when all would know Yahweh.

The New Covenant

The Sinai covenant was conditional on the people's ability to obey the Law—and the people had failed to obey. Jeremiah now foresees a whole new basis for covenant. What is new is that there is a change in the manner in which the divine will is to be conveyed to the people. Yahweh is to by-pass the process of speaking and listening and project a new vision of himself: a God of compassion and mercy and overwhelming love. Jeremiah's own experience is reflected here. He had preached to a hopelessly obdurate people; he is convinced that God must take a hand and change the human heart (cf. 32:37-41). He glimpses the era of the Spirit as Paul will characterise it—the 'law of the Spirit of life' (Rom 8:2).

The greatest tribute to Jeremiah was paid by the one whose way he had prepared. On that night before the Lord went to his death, he brought the most solemn promise of the prophet to fulfilment: 'This cup is the new covenant in my blood' (Lk 22:20). God had set his seal on the life and message of his servant.

A Prophet for our Day

Jeremiah has particular relevance for our day. His pre-decessors, as far as we know, accepted their prophetic mission with submissiveness—Isaiah indeed with eagerness (Is 6:9). But Jeremiah had to question; there is in him a trace of rebellion. He was not at all satisfied to accept, uncritically, traditional theological positions. He struggled, as the author of Job was to do centuries later, with the problem of retribution (12:1) and asserted the principle of individual (as against collective) responsibility (31:29-30). But, mostly, it was his own prophetic office that was his burden, and it was indeed a burden far heavier and more painful than that of any other prophet. He needed, all the more, the support of his God. His obedience was so much the greater because of his questioning, because he felt its yoke, because it led to a feeling of being abandoned.

There is no doubt that Jeremiah could be outspoken—as here:

O Lord, you have deceived me, and I was deceived; you
are stronger than I, and you have prevailed. I have become
a laughing-stock all the day; everyone mocks me (20:7).

This is truly marvellous. Let us look at what Jeremiah implies
when he declares: 'you are stronger than I'. What he says in
effect is: 'Yahweh, you are a great big bully!' He has had it up
to *here*. And he tells his God so in no uncertain terms. For
Jeremiah, his God is so real, so personal, that he can speak out
to him—and at him—with outrageous boldness. The decisive
factor is that Jeremiah can do so from a position of strength.
He is a prophet who, no matter how hard it went, was unflinch-
ingly faithful to the service his God had asked of him.

We see a Jeremiah at his wits' end. He wanted to pack it all
in:

If I say, 'I will no longer mention him, or speak any more
in his name,' there is in my heart as it were a burning fire
shut up in my bones, and I am weary with holding it in,
and I cannot (20:9).

While the prophet is doubtless thinking of the urgency of the
prophetic word, his cry will find an echo in the heart of any man
or woman who serves the Lord in a painful situation. It is never
easy to bear witness in face of repulse. It is so much more
difficult in face of blank indifference. Why not just pack one's
bags and slip away? Only a profound conviction of vocation
can hold one to the task. It is consoling to know that even a
Jeremiah could contemplate 'changing his option'!

EZEKIEL—*Prophet of the Temple*

The Jews exiled in Babylon were the cream of Judah: its
political, ecclesiastical and intellectual leaders. This explains
why the total (4,600 adult males) given in an appendix to
Jeremiah (Jer 52:28-30) is so restricted. They lived in special
settlements near Babylon and their lot was not unduly hard.

Indeed, there was opportunity for economic advancement and many of them did so well that they elected to remain on in Babylon after Cyrus had opened the way for a return to Palestine. It was inevitable that some of them, their faith shattered by the terrible disaster that had befallen their nation, were won over by Babylonian culture. But others clung more closely to their past. Encouraged, first by Ezekiel and then by Second Isaiah, they were buoyed up by fresh hope.

Ezekiel, son of Buzi, and a priest at Jerusalem was, with the king Jehoiachin and other prominent citizens of Judah, carried off to Babylon in the first of three deportations (597 BC; Ezek 1:1-3). His ministry falls into two periods: from 593 to the fall of Jerusalem (587) and from the fall of the city to 571, the date of his last recorded oracle (29:17-20). During the first part of his ministry, Ezekiel's message was very like that of Jeremiah. It might be summarised like this:

> The people of Israel are gravely culpable. God is just and is preparing to punish them. Very soon the siege of Jerusalem and the deportation will show what an intervention of Yahweh means.

In one respect, however, Ezekiel differs notably from Isaiah and Jeremiah: when he speaks of sin he has not in mind transgression of the social and moral commandments but cultic offences. For him, the cause of Judah's approaching fall lay in failure in the sphere of the holy. The nation had defiled the sanctuary (5:11), had turned aside to other cults (8:7-18), and had taken idols to its heart (14:3-11); in a word, the nation had 'rendered itself unclean' in the eyes of Yahweh. The great allegories of chapters 16 and 23 and the historical retrospect of chapter 20 are emphatic on this score. There can be no mistaking the priestly point of view. Though truly a prophet, Ezekiel's roots were in the tradition of the priesthood. So, the standards by which he measured Israel's conduct were the 'ordinances' and the 'judgements' which Yahweh had given to his people (5:6; 18:5-9; 33:25). Priestly tradition coloured his preaching, and his great vision of the future (40-48)—though much of it may not be from Ezekiel himself—is aptly called the torah of Ezekiel.

The Nation

The three historical reviews (chs 16; 20; 23) hold not only cultic interest; they occupy a special place in Israel's conception of its history. Granted, the allegories are lengthy and repetitious and the language is consciously crude. Ezekiel seemed to wish to say all that could be said about Israel's unfaithfulness, its indifference to the love of God, and its utter failure to obey. The picture he painted could scarcely be blacker than it is. But we need to keep in mind that he was justifying the divine chastisement which would fall in the near future: even divine patience had at last run out. We need also to observe that the prophet pointed to God's saving will—now more than ever seen to be free and unmerited (cf. 16:60-63; 20:40-44). In this sense, the three sombre chapters are the prelude to the glory of Yahweh's deed, for it is evident that his salvation cannot be based on any good in Israel itself. Paul will follow much the same technique when, on a broader canvas, he will paint, in black, the sinful helplessness of humankind, as a background to God's incredibly gracious saving deed in Christ (Rom 1-8).

The Individual

Ezekiel was concerned not only with the nation but with the individual too. At this time the old conception of a man's guilt being incurred by his whole family, especially by his children who had to answer for it, was proving inadequate (cf. Jer 31:29; Ezek 18:2). the celebrated vision of the sins of Jerusalem (Ezek 8-11) provided Ezekiel with the elements of a solution; he develops these and proclaims the moral principles in chapter 18 (cf. ch. 35). From these principles a fundamental religious truth, belief in retribution after death, will one day be deduced—but that day is centuries in the future. In the meantime, the prophet showed himself the champion of individual responsibility. True, this idea was not absent from Yahwism before his time. It was present, vaguely at least, from the beginning, but now it received powerful expression:

> The one who has sinned is the one who must die; a son is not to bear his father's guilt, nor a father his son's guilt; the righteousness of the righteous shall be his alone, and the wickedness of the wicked shall be his alone (18:20).

The Sentinel

Ezekiel was called to be a 'watcher' for the house of Israel, a pastor of his people (33:1-9). He had not only to deliver the divine 'word' or prophecy; he was also like a sentinel on the city wall who would warn the people of approaching danger, who would give Israel a chance to 'turn', to repent. He saw his pastoral office as not just an extension of his prophetic calling; rather, it became his duty to live for other people, to seek them out and to place himself at their disposal. His words were designed to give comfort and hope to the individual and to demonstrate that Yahweh desires only repentance and obedience. When the heaviness of divine judgment brought his exiled people to the verge of despair, he faced the problem squarely. He faced the alternatives of life and death: one lives by righteousness, one dies through sin. A person is free to choose between the two and the open door to the choice is repentance (33:10-20). The exiles are to live by Yahweh's word—he will perform his promised works (12:24-5). It was Ezekiel's pastoral concern to help his people to see themselves as they really were and to know their God as he truly is. Then right relations would be restored and he would be their God in earnest and they would be his people indeed.

The Good Shepherd

Ezekiel had a sublime vision of the majesty of God, one notably influenced by the priestly tradition to which he was heir. Yahweh is exalted above all creation, enthroned in majesty above his universe. No words can describe him. He is the holy one, transcendent, rather remote; hence the prophet's insistence on a worthy cult. Yet, at the same time he saw this God as redeemer. In a moving chapter (34) Yahweh is portrayed as the good shepherd who cares for his sheep, who performs the function of the righteous ruler, who searches for the lost in dark ravines and who finds for them fresh pasture. The Johannine Jesus consciously echoed the thought and imagery of Ezekiel (Jn 10:11-15). Hence, Ezekiel's call for a sincere conversion to Yahweh, for a new heart and a new spirit, pointed to a personal God, a God who is intensely present. His insistence on the need of interior religion indicates a personal

66

relationship with God which, if not as movingly expressed as it is by Jeremiah, is nonetheless very real.

New Heart, New Spirit

In the promise of a new heart and a new spirit (36:23-8) the prophet echoes Jeremiah 31:31-4. Here, too, the purpose of God's saving activity is the re-creation of a people capable of obeying the commandments perfectly. 'A new heart I will give you, and a new spirit I will put within you; and I will take out of your flesh the heart of stone and give you a heart of flesh' (Ezek 36:26). Thus equipped with a new heart and the bestowal of the Spirit, Israel will be able to walk in the path of the divine ordinances. What, in an Irish context, that prayer for a 'new heart' might mean is brought out by Sean O'Casey in his *Juno and the Paycock*. Mrs Boyle mourns a victim of civil war: 'Sacred Heart o' Jesus, take away our hearts o' stone, and give us hearts o'flesh! take away this murdherin' hate, an' give us Thine own eternal love!' A prayer, sadly, still needful in a civil war more than half a century later.

Ezekiel's promise of salvation is prefaced by the words: 'It is not for your sake, O house of Israel, that I am about to act, but for the sake of my holy name' (36:22). This is a recurring thought: that by gathering Israel and bringing it back to its own land, Yahweh manifests his holiness in the sight of the nations (20:41; 28:25; 36:23). Israel, by its infidelity, had profaned the name of its God before the nations; now God owes it to his honour that the covenant should be re-established. But there is more to it than that. Many of the predictions of coming events conclude with the words: 'that they may know that I am Yahweh'. The final goal of divine activity is that Yahweh should be recognised and worshipped by those who have never known him, or who do not know him as he is. And God is the God of forbearance and love.

The New Temple

The last nine chapters of Ezekiel (40-48) not only describe exactly the New Temple and its rites, but go on to describe the division of the country among the sanctuary, the prince, and the twelve tribes. In effect, it is a dream: an ideal picture of the wished-for reorganisation of the community after the Exile.

These chapters, from our viewpoint neither very interesting nor very intelligible, have really had more influence than the rest of the book. They give expression to a political and religious ideal that, in large measure, was to mark emerging Judaism. In a sense, the present conclusion, 48:30-35, a later addition, may have caught, accurately and strikingly, the spirit of chapters 40-48. The passage described the walls and gates of the ideal city and reveals its name: 'And the name of the city henceforth shall be, The Lord is there' (v.35).

'The city's essential characteristic, conferring upon it its real importance in the history of God's dealing with his people, is that all-important characteristic of the Temple which was revealed to Ezekiel in the vision constituting the core of chapters 40-48, and which is developed in the rest of the material progressively added to that core: God's earthly presence is focussed there.... The old faithless city is no more, and the new one will be radically different. So radical a change calls for abandonment of the old name, Jerusalem, and conferment of a new name which will fit the city's new character better. The vital element in the city's new character, the transcendental fact which will determine its place in the future history of the whole house of Israel, is expressed in the city's symbolic new name: "The Lord is there". We do not know whether Ezekiel with his earthly eyes ever saw the city of his origins rising from its ruins. Perhaps that no longer mattered to him. He had already seen God's glory there, with the eyes of a visionary.'[5]

JONAH—*Reluctant Prophet*

Despite the glowing poetic promise of Second Isaiah (Is 40-55), return from the Babylonian Exile was on a depressingly small scale. In the tiny Jewish state of the fifth century the struggle to preserve national identity was painful. It is understandable that, among the returned exiles and their descendants, in view of all they had been through and were still suffering, a certain exclusiveness, a ghetto-mentality, should have appeared—at least in some circles. Those who shared this outlook wished to cut themselves off from contact with other peoples and looked with impatience for the judgment of God on the Gentiles. The book of Jonah is a criticism of this stance and a bold declaration that God is the God of all peoples. It is no naïve collection of improbable miracles but is a highly sophisticated piece of writing, a brilliant satire. Though listed among the twelve minor prophets, Jonah is not a prophetical writing at all. It is a work of fiction, attached to the name of an eighth-century prophet briefly mentioned in 2 Kings 14:25—Jonah, son of Amittai—and was written most likely in the fourth century.

The Reluctant Prophet

The Jonah of the book is presented as a prophet of the Chosen People. He was called to preach to the Assyrians, the hated oppressors of his people—Assyrian oppressors in keeping with the eighth-century background. The prophet well knew the mercy of his God and he suspected that, in fact, the Assyrians would repent and that God would not carry out his threat against them: 'Yet forty days, and Nineveh shall be overthrown!' (Jon 3:4). The thought of divine mercy extended to the great enemy was more than Jonah could stomach. Instead of setting out for Nineveh in the east, he fled to the west, 'from the presence of the Lord' (1:1-3). The famous 'great fish' of 1:17; 2:10 is no more than an 'executive submarine' to get Jonah back on the job!

With splendid artistry the author contrasts the narrow, unforgiving disposition of the Israelite prophet with the open and sympathetic attitude of the other actors in his story—all Gentiles. The pagan sailors are horrified to learn that anyone can bring oneself to disobey a divine command (1:10) and they are loath to cast him into the raging sea—his own suggested means of restoring calm (1:12). The king of Nineveh and his people at once believe the word of the prophet and are converted and do penance (3:6-99). The irony is unmistakable: the preaching of the reluctant Jonah meets with an immediate and universal response in the pagan city whereas the great prophets had, over the centuries, preached to the Chosen People in vain!

The Gracious God

God did accept the sincere conversion of the Ninevites; but what of Jonah? 'It displeased Jonah exceedingly and he was angry' (4:1). Naïvely, he complains that this is precisely why he had fled to the west: 'for I knew that you are a gracious God, and merciful, slow to anger, and abounding in steadfast love' (v.2). His worst fear is realised. Still, he did not quite give up hope that the Lord might again change his mind and he sat outside the city, waiting for the desired destruction (4:5). God, patient even with his stubborn prophet, taught him a gentle but effective lesson. He caused a plant to spring up and give shade to a Jonah stolidly sitting out under a burning sun and then permitted it to wither just as quickly—to the chagrin of the prophet (4:6-9). The moral of the lesson is made clear: if Jonah felt that he had a right to feel annoyed because the plant had shrivelled up, should not God pity Nineveh in which there were more than 120,000 helpless infants—'who do not know their right hand from their left' (4:11)—as well as many animals, and not destroy it? The loving mercy of God extends to all peoples and to all his creatures.

The 'great fish' should never have figured as *the* problem of Jonah. Much more striking is the fantastic dimensions given to the city: 'Nineveh was an exceedingly great city, three days' journey in breadth' (3:3); Jonah felt he had not really arrived in the city until he had walked for a whole day across it (v.4). The immense number of infants would suit the population of such a megapolis. Most remarkable of all is the conversion of king and people. It is formally stated that the people of Nineveh believed God (3:5), and God himself acknowledged the sincerity of their conversion (3:10). The literal-minded will question the 'fish', will challenge, on archaeological grounds, the size and population of Nineveh and, on historical grounds, the conversion of the Assyrians. Those who listen to story will take it all in their stride. For they will see in it the God who is caring Father of all—and hear in it a stark challenge. The challenge is that of Jesus himself: 'Love your enemy!'.

In the varied wisdom literature of the Old Testament two books stand apart: Job and Qoheleth (Ecclesiastes). Their authors are theological rebels, taking a firm stand against a position that otherwise went unquestioned. Theirs was the not uncommon fate of such bold questioners—to be ignored in their own day (better, perhaps, than being accused of 'dissent'). Time was to vindicate the truth of their perception. They are congenial figures, or, it may be, encouraging figures, in the theological climate of our day.

The Book of Job (probably dating from the beginning of the fifth century BC) belongs to the stage when the idea of individual retribution in this life palpably ran up against insoluble practical difficulties. For an understanding not only of this book but of the great bulk of the wisdom literature, it is important to remind ourselves that the Hebrews had a very vague notion of the afterlife. At death a person did not quite disappear but continued to exist in some dim, undefined way in Sheol; but in that dismal abode of the dead all, rich and poor, good and bad, were equal. Given this situation, it is inevitable that, throughout most of the Old Testament, retribution of good or evil was seen in an exclusively earthly perspective, strictly within the confines of this life. It was not until the beginning of the second century BC—two centuries or so later than the book of Job—that the doctrine of retribution after death made its appearance (the earliest biblical reference being Dan 12:2). Until that point was reached it had to be (if there be justice at all) that both good and wicked must find their just deserts *here on earth,* and the received theology stoutly maintained that such indeed was the case. But progress was made by troubled souls (cf. Ezek 18:2; Jer 31:29; Mal 2:17) searching for a solution that was truly the measure of reality. The Book of Job marks the longest stride in that progress.

The Patience of Job?

Job has become a figure of proverbial patience but anyone who has troubled to read the book of Job may well be at a loss to understand how he came by such a reputation. After all, he curses the day of his birth in no uncertain terms (ch.3) and more than once he practically serves God an ultimatum. But what if there are two Jobs? This, indeed, is more or less the case. The author of the book found his inspiration in a story about a legendary Edomite sheik who, when tried by Satan—not yet the evil spirit of later biblical tradition—proved unshakeably faithful. On the basis of this story Israel's greatest poet built his masterpiece.

The prose sections (Prologue and Epilogue, 1:1-2:13; 42:7-14) no doubt do reflect a popular story—but one that has been rewritten by the author of Job. And that story, naïve as it may seem, is an essential part of the work. As a matter of fact, it is vitally important for an understanding of Job. Job protests his innocence while his friends are convinced of his sinfulness. Who is in the right, they or he? Without the Prologue we would have no means of knowing. But this prologue puts the reader in the picture. The trials of Job follow on a wager between God and Satan. Twice (1:8; 2:3) God acknowledges the righteousness of 'my servant Job'; twice Job's steadfastness is asserted (1:22; 2:10). And the Epilogue, with its description of the restoration of Job's fortunes, is a vindication of his righteousness. The reader is left in no doubt.

Job's Problem

In the dialogues Job wrestles with a tormenting problem: he is suffering, yet knows himself to be innocent. The inadequacy of the traditional view (the traditional doctrine of retribution, in its simplest form, is that the good are rewarded and the wicked are punished *in this life*) has become apparent, but people can close their eyes to a disturbing new truth. Here the three friends (Eliphaz, Bildad and Zophar) are the champions of 'orthodoxy'. They have accepted the classic teaching without question and quite refuse to admit that it will not fit the facts of the present case. Their position is very simple: suffering is punishment for sin; if a man suffers it is because he is a sinner. The facts must be made to fit the traditional viewpoint! Hence they proceed to comfort the sufferer by insisting that he must be a sinner—and a great sinner at that, to judge by his sufferings—and they grow more insistent as he protests his innocence.

The author has brilliantly sustained the contrast between

two irreconcilable theological positions. Indeed, he has shown how Job and his friends drift further apart. And, perhaps not without some malice, he shows that while they become more and more sure of themselves, Job becomes more and more open to God. In particular, the way of Eliphaz, the senior of the comforters, is a satirical comment on theological intransigence. At first Eliphaz, serene in theological rectitude, is the soul of benignity towards a benighted Job. And he is sure that the sufferer will—must—listen to sweet reason. Job is being rightfully punished for his sin; but let him take heart:

> Behold, happy is the man whom God reproves;
> therefore despise not the chastening of the Almighty
> (5:17).

He has no doubt as to the lot of a repentant Job:

> You shall come to your grave in ripe old age (5:26).

In the second discourse Eliphaz is petulant. Really, this is too much: Job has dared to question the wisdom of his friends, he has challenged their theology. Who does he think he is indeed:

> What do you know that we do not know?
> What do you understand that is not clear to us? (16:9).

However, Eliphaz is still determined to help, to demonstrate to Job the error of his ways:

> I will show you, hear me;
> and what I have seen I will declare (15:17).

But Job will not be taught. He still dares to protest his innocence, still will not acknowledge the 'truth'. For Eliphaz *knows* that he is right: his theology tells him so. With hair-raising self-assurance he not only insists on Job's guilt but cooly examines Job's conscience for him, cataloguing his crimes: he is a usurer and an exploiter of the poor, a man insensitive to the misery of others (22:5-11). Eliphaz, we know, will remain unmoved by Job's vehement rebuttal of his charges (ch. 31). It matters not at all that Job *is* innocent in God's sight. By the standard of human theology he is clearly in the wrong.

73

Job's Protest

But Job does protest and continues to protest. He *knows* that he is innocent; at least he is certain that he has done nothing to deserve such trials. His world has broken in pieces about him for he, too, had subscribed to the traditional doctrine. Now he sees that it does not meet his case—but he has no other solution. He struggles manfully with his problem but there is no way out. His sufferings are now utterly meaningless and he is tempted to question the justice of God.

> How long will you not look away from me,
> nor let me alone till I swallow my spittle? (7:19).
> Behold, he will slay me; I have no hope;
> yet I will defend my ways to his face (13:15).
> He has kindled his wrath against me,
> and counts me as his adversary (19:11).

This Job is not the improbable hero of the older tale but a man of flesh and blood, striving to find a glimmer of meaning in the inscrutable ways of God, a man groping in thick darkness—but it is the darkness of faith. The grandeur of Job is that he can 'defy the sufferings which overwhelm him to rob him of his faith in a hidden God'. There is another dimension, too, to Job's protest.

Israel, though people of Yahweh, had absorbed much of the 'common theology' of the Ancient Near East. That theology envisaged an ordered world, and upheld that order. Readily, this cosmic order was held to legitimate political order. Legitimation of structure, defence of the status quo, became a major function of theology—markedly so in the Judaean theology of David and the Temple. But there were voices of protest. There was the suspicion that God did not necessarily stand over the structure, there was a recognition that political and religious power could be oppressive. There was challenge not only of the structure but of the God who allegedly upheld the structure. This was a decisive turning which found expression in Israel's practice of lament.

'The moment when Israel found the nerve and the faith to risk an assault on the throne of God with complaint was a decisive moment against legitimation. The lament is a dramatic, rhetorical, liturgical act of speech which makes clear that Israel will no longer be a submissive, subservient recipient of decrees from the throne. There is a bold movement and voice from Israel's side which does not blindly and docilely accept, but means to have its dengerous say, even in the face of God'[6] It was a recognition that Israel's God was not a God who would brook no challenge but one who can be directly challenged. A God, indeed, who invited challenge. Job is an outstanding spokesman of challenge.

The extraordinarily harsh protest of 9:19-24 decisively nullifies the dominant theology. Job definitely concludes that the theology of legitimated structure does not work:

> If it is a contest of strength, behold him!
> If it is a matter of justice, who can summon him?
> Though I am innocent, my own mouth would condemn
> me;
> though I am blameless, he would prove me perverse...
> It is all one; therefore I say,
> he destroys both the blameless and the wicked.
> When disaster brings sudden death,
> he mocks at the calamity of the innocent.

There is an even more outrageous passage—24:1-12. Job asks in exasperation: 'Why are not times of judgement kept by the Almighty?' Then he describes the arrogant oppression of the oppressor and the helpless suffering of the oppressed. It is an intolerably unjust situation. At the end he hurls his challenge at God:

> From out of the city the dying groan,
> and the soul of the wounded cries for help;
> yet God pays no attention to their prayer.

The sheer honesty is heart-rending. How utterly different it is from another view:

> I was young and now I am old,
> but I have never seen the just man forsaken
> nor his children begging for bread (Ps 37:25).

This is pathetic: a desperate clinging to a doctrinaire position in face of the evidence. But if your theology is a strict theology of structure legitimation, then you must, perforce, sacrifice fact to theory.

75

My Servant Job

What is God's assessment of a thoroughly rebellious Job? It is unambiguous. The three staunch champions of the 'common theology' fare very badly indeed. They had upheld the honour of Yahweh against the 'blasphemer'. To their shock, Yahweh supports the outrageous Job and condemns their righteousness. Surely an anticipation of Jesus' view of things.

> The Lord said to Eliphaz the Temanite: 'My wrath is kindled against you and your two friends; for you have not spoken of me what is right, as my servant Job has' (42:7).

QOHELETH—*the Goad*

The Book of Qoheleth (Ecclesiastes) comes after Job and marks a development. Once again the problem of personal retribution is taken up and once again the traditional doctrine is found wanting. This is not to say that the position of Job is just restated in more emphatic terms—it is not at all a parallel treatment of the matter. Job was able to show that suffering does not presuppose sin in the sufferer and can be quite independent of guilt; but what about the reward of the virtuous? It is precisely this other side of the picture, the view that the just must be happy, that Qoheleth questions. He observes that when a person, even a righteous person, has all that that person wants, it does not bring contentment. Now, at last, the inadequacy of the received theology had been well and truly challenged but the time was not yet ripe for the break that would provide a more satisfactory answer. In the meantime, even so gifted a sage as ben Sirach (author of Ecclesiasticus) would take the 'orthodox' view for granted. Qoheleth is of a different cast: he refuses to take a mechanical view of Providence. For him God is no accountant keeping a rigid balance sheet and doling out life and death, happiness and misery, in strict proportion to one's virtue or guilt. God is in no way answerable to men and women.

A Cold Eye

Qoheleth—the name means a speaker or preacher—casts a cold eye on human life and he does not flinch from what he sees there. He has the courage to admit that the things which are supposed to satisfy us do not satisfy us. He tests our customary values and finds them wanting. Pleasure is not the answer (2:1-11): 'I said of laughter, "It is mad", and of pleasure, "What use is it?"' This is the disillusion of one who has everything, an ailment of affluent society. Fulfilment is not to be found in wisdom (2:12-17). It is true that wisdom excels folly as light excels darkness. The wise man walks with wide-open eyes, while the fool stumbles in the dark. Yet, there is the irony of the situation: the wise man dies just as readily as the fool. As for work (2:18-23)—one must, inevitably, leave the fruit of one's toil to another, and whether that other be wise or a fool, one cannot really know. The traditional theology of retribution satisfies Qoheleth no more than it does Job. Qoheleth unmasks its inadequacy: 3:16; 6:3; 7:15. 'There is a vanity which takes place on earth, that there are righteous men to whom it happens according to the deeds of the wicked, and there are wicked men to whom it happens according to the deeds of the righteous. I said that this also is vanity' (8:14). None of this is very comforting—except for the comfort of realism. And the candid Qoheleth has the courage of his conviction: he throws down the gauntlet to his peers, questioning their academic pretension:

> When I applied my mind to know wisdom ... then I saw all the work of God, that man cannot find out the work that is done under the sun. However much man may toil in his seeking, he will not find it out; even though a wise man claims to know, he cannot find it out (8:16-17).

Such bluntness cannot have won him popularity. This is wryly admitted by the editor responsible for the Epilogue, (12:9-14): 'The sayings of the wise are like goads' (12:1). He wonders aloud whether it might have been better if such an uncomfortable book had not been written: 'Of making many books there is no end' (12:12).

Life

If everything in life is vanity, then life itself is a riddle. The after-life cannot offer its solution to the riddle, because there is no after-life. The problem of existence must be answered within the brief span between birth and death. Here, too, Qoheleth is the realist. Life is not, or is not always, full of pain, a cruel joke. If there is vanity and pain there is also meaning and joy. One must thankfully take the smooth with the rough: 'In the day of prosperity be joyful, and in the day of adversity consider; God has made the one as well as the other' (7:14). One must count one's blessings. This is all the more important when one cannot lift one's gaze beyond the horizons of this life. The apparently hedonistic recommendations of Qoheleth are nothing other than a thorough-going acceptance of the essential goodness of God's creation: 'There is nothing better for a man than that he should eat and drink and find enjoyment in his toil. This also, I saw, is from the hand of God' (2:24). Life is short and too precious to be wasted; we have only one life and we should make the most of it: 'Whatever your heart finds to do, do it with all your might; for there is no work or thought or knowledge in Sheol, to which you are going' (9:10). And life is precious, so precious in contrast to the meaningless-ness of death: 'He who is joined with all the living has hope, for a living dog is better than a dead lion. For the living know that they will die, but the dead know nothing' (9:4-5).

Death

It is obvious that the question of death hangs like a dark shadow over the whole book. Life ends in death—whether life be a tissue of pain or one with its measure of fulfilment. This is the ultimate vanity. Qoheleth describes death in terms of Genesis 2:7—'The dust returns to the earth as it was, and the spirit returns to God who gave it' (Qoh 12:7). The human person is effectively dissolved. Indeed, Qoheleth can find no distinction between man and beast in this respect:

> For the fate of the sons of men and the fate of beasts is the same; as one dies, so dies the other. They all have the same breath, and the man has no advantage over the beasts, for all is vanity. All go to one place; all are from the dust, and

78

all turn to dust again. Who knows whether the spirit of man goes upward and the spirit of the beast goes down to the earth (3:19-21).

The point he makes—and how effectively he makes it—is that death is the great leveller. He is thoroughly biblical in his conviction that humankind is the summit of God's creation, standing apart from and above all other creatures (Gen 1-2). And yet there is the inescapable fact that man and beast meet in death. Let us recall that Sheol is a place of darkness and gloom, away from the sight of God. In this perspective we can judge the grandeur of the faith of Qoheleth. He has looked on life and death and he has had the honesty to acknowledge that, from a human point of view, both the one and the other are vanity. But his faith reaches beyond human confines to God, and like Job, in God he finds the answer to his problem.

Faith

Qoheleth has had the courage to question and to challenge because his vantage point is one of faith. He questions not because he doubts but because faith is a path through darkness: humankind cannot know the work of God. And, at the end of all, Qoheleth is content to acknowledge that, because God *is* in his heaven, all is well with the world. He is content to leave it all in the hands of his God: 'I know that whatever God does endures forever; nothing can be added to it, nor anything taken from it' (3:14). All that God has made is good, the whole of creation—though so much is riddlesome—has a marvellous purposefulness: 'He has made everything beautiful in its time' (3:11). Here is indeed the Creator who had looked with complacency upon his creation and had entrusted this earth to humankind for our benefit, the God who bears patiently with an ungrateful and rebellious humankind. The most important thing in life is to stand right with God; this is the strong conviction of Qoheleth: 'I know that it will be well with those who fear God, because they fear before him' (8:12). Throughout, Qoheleth is the realist. And in the last analysis he is something more. He has plunged more deeply still into the dark labyrinth uncovered by Job and he too, despite his vain searchings for an outlet, clings desperately to his faith in God.

No more than Job does he solve his problem, but he has cleared the way by contesting illusory solutions. Qoheleth challenged his contemporaries to think. He did not provide answers but he raised questions which, some day, had to be faced.

The pilgrimage of the authors of Job and of Qoheleth was a journey of the mind and of the spirit. They were explorers, no longer content to walk a well-defined road. They suspected that the familiar road led nowhere. Though none would follow, they struck out. They did not get to the end but they did challenge complacency. The well-trodden way was not the only way.

They discovered that their God did not hurl thunderbolts at those who dared to question and to protest. They learned that he does not provide ready answers to life's riddles. They perceived that human solutions are too often illusory. In their way they anticipated the perception of Paul: 'The foolishness of God is wiser than men, and the weakness of God is stronger than men' (1 Cor 1:25). In their doubting and their questioning they came to a deeper knowledge of God: they found the true God. Now they could step, trustfully, into the unknown.

ESTHER—*Reluctant Heroine*

The story of Esther (second century BC) tells how a beautiful young Jewess, guided by her wise uncle Mordecai—she was an orphan—had become queen of the Persians (Esther 2:1-17). The tale opens with a lavish banquet given by King Ahasuerus (Xerxes) in the course of which he had the notion to display the great beauty of his queen, Vashti. She was not amused and refused point-blank to be made a show of before a crowd of drunken men—the banquet was in its seventh day. Crisis stations. The king was bluntly advised: 'This deed of the queen will be made known to all women, causing them to look with contempt upon their husbands, since they will say, "King Ahasuerus commanded Queen Vashti to be brought before him, and she did not come".' (1:17). Something had to be done, at once. Accordingly it was decreed that the king should promptly divorce his disobedient queen. And the new queen would be chosen on the basis of a beauty contest (2:2-4). This cleared the way for the rise of Esther. It was inevitable that the lovely Jewish maiden (her Jewishness was not disclosed) should be winner: 'the king loved Esther more than all the women, and she found grace and favour in his sight more than all the virgins, so that he set the royal crown on her head and made her queen instead of Vashti' (2:17).

The stage is set: enter the villain—Haman the grand-vizier. He was mortally offended by the sturdy independence of Mordecai (Esther's uncle and guardian) who pointedly refused to bow down or do obeisance to the grand-vizier. Haman plotted his revenge, and not on Mordecai alone. He persuaded the king to proclaim a pogrom of all Jews throughout the Persian empire (3:7-15). Mordecai saw that there was but one hope of escape for the Jews: the good offices of Esther. He persuaded a reluctant queen that she must plead with the king for her people. He pointed out that her unexpected station was providential: 'Who knows whether you have not come to the kingdom for such a time as this?' (4:14). Esther yielded, but not before he had agreed to her terms that all Jews in the Persian capital of Susa would hold a solemn fast for three days (4:15-17).

Save me from my Fear

Before taking the fateful step of approaching the king uninvited—for dramatic effect it is supposed that for anyone to approach the king without having been summoned means death (4:11)—Esther, 'seized with deadly anxiety, fled to the Lord' (14:1). The first part of her long prayer (14:3-19) is a typical 'prayer of the chastened' (14:3-14). Esther goes on to protest that her royal station is not of her choosing. She has no joy in being queen; her only joy is in the Lord: 'Your servant has no joy since the day that I was brought here until now, except in you, O Lord God of Abraham. O God, whose might is over all, hear the voice of the despairing, and save me from the hands of evildoers. And save me from my fear' (14:18-19). 'And save me from my fear!'. What a moving plea. Esther is no heroine who boldly takes a drastic step, as Judith will. She does what she knows is expected of her, but with no great enthusiasm. Her only hope now is in the help of her God. And her God did not fail her. What took place is related with charm.

The queen had prayed and fasted, clad in sackcloth. At the end of the third day, she arrayed herself in her most splendid robes. Then, accompanied by two of her maids, in trepidation, she made her way to the king: 'she looked happy, as if beloved, but her heart was frozen with fear'. Passing through door after door she was at last in the presence of the king and faced his fierce anger at the unwonted intrusion. She promptly fainted. 'Then God changed the spirit of the king to gentleness, and in alarm he sprang from his throne and took her in his arms until she came to herself. And he comforted her with soothing words, and said to her, "What is it, Esther? I am your brother. Take courage; you shall not die, for the law applies only to the people. Come near."' (15:8-9). She responded with words of flattery: 'I saw you, my lord, like an angel of God, and my heart was shaken with fear at your glory. For you are wonderful, my lord, and your countenance is full of grace' (15:13-14). And promptly fainted again! 'And the king was agitated, and all his servants sought to comfort her' (v.16). She knew when she was on to a good thing. From now on, Esther is invincible. With her to speak for them, her people are no longer in danger. The all-powerful monarch, king of kings, is putty in the delicate hands of a Jewish maiden. It is wishful thinking, of course; yet it must have brought some comfort to the heart of a subject people. (ch. 15).

As the story continues to unfold, Esther invites Haman to a banquet and denounces him to the king as one who was contriving to destroy her and her people. Haman ends up on the gallows he has prepared for Mordecai (ch. 7). The edict against the Jews is revoked and it is they who now strike down their enemies (ch. 9).

Purim

The Book of Esther was written to justify the feast of Purim, a feast that was not of Israelite origin and had no religious significance. It seems clear that the feast originated in the communities of the eastern Diaspora, perhaps at Susa. It probably commemorates a pogrom (some time in the fourth century BC) from which Jews escaped in a seemingly miraculous manner. The sentiments of the book are an understandable reaction to the hostility encountered by Jews—a feature of the ancient world as of later ages. The author is not describing historical events. The bloody massacre of enemies (9:5-17) never did take place, and Jews living in ghettoes throughout the hellenistic world were aware that it had not happened. Ultimately, the message of Esther is that God does not abandon his people. The remarkable feature is a story of deliverance dependent on the mediation of a woman.

JUDITH—*Mulier Fortis*

In the story of Judith—name means 'Jewess'—a down-trodden people gave expression, around the turn of the first century BC, to its dream of deliverance. Again, as with Esther, it is remarkable that the deliverer is a woman. In the story, the Jewish nation is in deadly danger. Holofernes, with his mighty Assyrian army, is besieging the town of Bethulia (Judith 7:1-3) which, for the purpose of the story, guarded the only way of access to Jerusalem. If Bethulia falls, the land is doomed. The author of Judith has gone out of his way to multiply historical and geographical howlers; he displays, according to the *Bible de Jérusalem,* 'a bland indifference to history and geography'. His object must have been to turn the attention of his readers from any precise historical context and bring it to bear only on the religious drama. Drama he has indeed achieved in the person and deed of a woman.

The disheartened defenders of Bethulia wanted to surrender but the governor, Uzziah, prevailed on them to postpone surrender for five days. If God had not acted by then, he would capitulate (7:23-31). Judith, a beautiful and virtuous widow, was appalled by such lack of confidence in God. She boldly upbraided the rulers of her people and read them a lesson in theology (8:9-27)—'Who are you that you have put God to the test this day, and are setting yourselves up in the place of God among the sons of men? You are putting the Lord Almighty to the test—but you will never know anything!' (8:12-13).

Shamefacedly, Uzziah agreed that Judith was right. There is, however, the embarassing problem that the besieged town was almost out of water! 'So pray for us, since you are a devout woman, and the Lord will send us rain to fill our cisterns and we will no longer be faint' (8:28-31). Judith is made of sterner metal than Esther and had already determined on a bold course of action. 'Listen to me. I am about to do a thing which will go down through all generations of our descendants. . . . Only, do not try to find out what I plan; for I will not tell you until I have finished what I am about to do' (8:32, 34). A resolute woman indeed.

Prayer

Judith was bold because her strength was in the Lord. 'Then Judith fell upon her face, and put ashes on her head, and uncovered the sackcloth she was wearing; and at the very time when the evening's incense was being offered in the house of God in Jerusalem, Judith cried out to the Lord with a loud voice' (9:1). She began: 'Give to me, a widow, the strength to do what I plan. By the deceit of my lips strike down the slave with the prince and the prince with his servant; crush their arrogance by the hand of a woman' (9:9-10). And she concludes with impassioned words:

> For your power depends not upon numbers, nor your might upon men of strength; for you are
> God of the lowly,
> helper of the oppressed,
> upholder of the weak,
> protector of the forlorn,
> saviour of those without hope.
> Hear, O hear me, God of my faith, God of the inheritance of Israel, Lord of heaven and earth, Creator of the waters, King of all creation, hear my prayer! Make my deceitful words to be their wound and stripe, for they have planned cruel things against your covenant, and against your consecrated house, and against the top of Zion, and against the house possessed by your children. And cause your whole nation and every tribe to know and understand that you are God, the God of all power and might, and

that there is no other who protects the people of Israel but you alone' (9:11-14).

Perhaps nowhere else is the faithful Israelite's sense of total dependence on God so forcefully expressed. Is it happy chance, or something else, that this lovely prayer is prayer of a woman?

By the Hand of a Woman

Judith began to put her plan into effect. First, she adorned herself 'and made herself very beautiful, to entice the eyes of all men who might see her' (10:4). As one who had always scrupulously observed the Law, she took care to pack an adequate supply of kosher food (10:5). Accompanied by a maid, Judith set out towards the enemy lines. They were promptly arrested by an Assyrian patrol—as she had intended they should be. She passed herself off as a deserter from the doomed town, one prepared to betray a secret way into the hill country, a means of taking Jerusalem with ease. Bemused by her beauty, the troops took her to their general; and her arrival in the camp caused quite a stir! Here, at its most blatant, is a theme that recurs in Hebrew stories, that of the remarkable beauty of Hebrew women: 'And they marvelled at her beauty, and admired the Israelites, judging them by her, and every one said to his neighbour, 'Who can despise these people, who have women like this among them? Surely not a man of them had better be left alive, for if we let them go they will be able to ensnare the whole world!''' (10:19). Holofernes, needless to say, was captivated, and swallowed her story (ch. 11).

Judith cleverly arranged that she and her maid could leave the camp at night, as they did three nights in a row, so preparing her escape route (ch. 12). On the fateful fourth night Holofernes held a banquet and invited Judith, planning to have his way with her afterwards. He was so happy at her presence that 'he drank a great quantity of wine, much more than he had ever drunk in any one day since he was born' (12:20). When Judith did, at last, find herself alone with the general, 'he was stretched out on his bed, for he was overcome with wine' (13:2). She was safe—and now was her chance to carry out her resolve. She laid hold of Holofernes' sword and with the cry, 'Give me strength this day, O Lord God of Israel' (v.7), struck off his head. With the severed head hidden in their food bag, she and her maid passed through the Assyrian outposts and came to Bethulia where they displayed undeniable proof of a mission accomplished (13:15). The author is careful to insist that not Judith's life only was guarded and has her declare: 'As the Lord has protected me in the way I went, it was my face that tricked him into his destruction, and yet he committed no act of sin with me, to defile and shame me' (13:16).

Uzziah was fulsome in his praise of the valiant Judith and blessed the God who had inspired her (13:18-20). With their general dead, the Assyrians panicked and were routed (chs 14-15). Judith became the toast of the nation. Joakim, the high priest, and 'the senate of the people of Israel' came from Jerusalem to greet her and sing her praises: 'You are the exaltation of Jerusalem, you are the great glory of Israel, you are the great pride of our nation!' (15:9). The long canticle of Judith (16:2-27) rounds off the dramatic story. For the greater part, it is a poetic version of her exploit but it runs on into a hymn of beauty (16:13-16) 'For every sacrifice as a fragrant offering is a small thing, and all fat for burnt offerings to you is a very little thing, but one who fears the Lord shall be great for ever' (v. 16). 'Fear of the Lord' is commitment to him, it is trustful service. This God of power and might holds no terror for his faithful ones. True greatness lies in serving him alone. It may be that it needs a woman to tell what faithfulness means.

Though Esther and Judith meet in the common theme of deliverance by a woman and though both illustrate the truth that God does not abandon his people, the two writings are really very different in outlook. The former is candidly nationalistic and expresses something of the exasperation of a ghetto mentality. Judith, on the other hand, is universalist in perspective. Significantly, the salvation of Jerusalem is achieved not in Judea but in Bethulia, in the land of the hated Samaritans. Even more striking, the religious issue of the conflict is brought out by Achior, an Ammonite (Judith 5:5-21), who is drawn to confess the true God (14:5-10). We have here an echo of Ruth and Jonah and already some of the atmosphere of that new age in which Jesus would hold up a Samaritan as a figure of Christian love (Lk 10:30-37) and would, raised from the earth, draw all to himself (Jn 12:32).

TOBIT—*a Fairy-tale*

The book of Tobit (around 200 BC) is concerned with a double case of the innocent sufferer. Tobit, meticulous in religious observance and magnanimous in his charity—a model Jew in short—is victim of an unfortunate accident. Sarah, an innocent girl, is grievously afflicted through no fault of hers. Both become the butt of bitter tongues (Tob 2:14; 3:8) and, as a result, both seek to die (3:6, 15). The key to the book is found in 3:16-17 and 12:12-15—the prayer of the two unhappy ones is presented to God by Raphael and the angel is entrusted with a mission to help them. A religious fairy-tale in short. The portrait of Azarias (the angel Raphael in human shape) is based on Gen 24:40—'He (Abraham) said to me: "The Lord before whom I walk will send his angel with you to prosper you on your way; and you shall take a wife for my son from my kindred".' Azarias is indeed an instrument of God's providence, a dramatic answer to prayer.

The modern reader will feel at home with this writing: it is a novel (with fairytale elements). The stories of Tobit and Sarah come together at 3:16-17—their separate prayers have met in the presence of God. With superb skill, the author traces the manner of God's response. Tobit (4:1) recalled that he had, years before, entrusted a sum of money to his friend Gabael and he now decided to send his son Tobias to claim it. To be his son's companion and guide on the journey he hired a Jew named Azarias (the reader knows that he is, in fact, the angel Raphael). The angel encouraged the young man in face of danger and helped him to procure a remedy for his father's blindness and also one against the machinations of evil spirits—thus he could deliver Sarah (6:1-8). Moreover, he so effectively extolled the charms of Sarah that Tobias, before ever he had set eyes on the girl, 'fell in love with her and lost his heart to her hopelessly' (6:17). At Ecbatana (in Persia) they visited the home of Raguel, kinsman of Tobit and father of Sarah. Tobias lost no time in seeking the girl's hand. And the story then moves towards its 'they lived happily ever after' ending.

But there was an obstacle to be overcome. A jealous demon, Asmodeus, had almost wrecked Sarah's life. She had been betrothed seven times and, each time, the demon had slain the unfortunate fiancé. Raguel had to cede to the earnest Tobias: 'He drew up the marriage contract and so gave his daughter as bride to Tobias according to the ordinance of the Law of Moses' (7:13). But he could not hide his apprehension. He quietly dug a grave so that, if the worst happened, Tobias might be secretly buried before daylight (8:9). He need not have worried. A maid sent to check found the young couple sleeping peacefully (8:12-13).

Marriage of True Love

Thanks to Azarias, Tobias had been able to cope with Asmodeus. When he and his bride had retired to their bedroom, Tobias did as the angel had instructed him. He burned some of the heart and liver of a great fish they had taken on this journey (6:2-6); the reek of it put the demon to flight. Before they retired, Tobias spoke to his bride: 'Sister [a term of endearment], let us pray that the Lord may have mercy on us' (8:4). This was in keeping with an admonishment of the angel (still in the context of protection against the demon): 'When you approach her, rise up, both of you, and cry out to the merciful God, and he will save you and have mercy on you' (6:17). Tobias prayed:

> Blessed are you, O God of our fathers.
> and blessed be your holy and glorious name forever.
> Let the heavens and all your creatures bless you.
> You made Adam and gave him Eve his wife
> as a helper and support.
> From them the race of humankind has sprung.
> You did say, 'It is not good that the man should be alone;
> let us make a helper for him like himself'.
> And now, O Lord, I am not taking this sister of mine
> because of lust, but with sincerity.
> Grant that I may find mercy
> and may grow old together with her.
> And she said with him, 'Amen, Amen'.
> Then they both lay down for the night. (8:5-9).

The prayer is manifestly inspired by Genesis 2:7-24. Both texts reflect the positive, healthy attitude of Israel to sex and marriage. This becomes all the more clear when we compare the moralising tone of the Vulgate text of Tobit. At 8:4 the Vulgate specifies that the prayer of the young couple lasted for three nights—and only then did the two sleep together. Already the Vulgate had spelled out its view, in the angel's admonition to Tobias (6:18-22)

> You shall take her, Sarah, into the chamber, and for three days keep yourself continent from her, and give yourself to nothing else but to prayers with her.... And when the third night is past, you shall take the virgin with the fear of the Lord, moved rather for love of children than for lust: that in the seed of Abraham you may obtain a blessing in children (6:18, 22).

Obviously, these Vulgate prescriptions mark a grave departure from the serenity of the earlier story. There Tobias echoes the inspiring and encouraging note of Genesis 2: the later additions strike an alien note. It is sad that, in Christian history, they have had the greater resonance. Tobit is in step with the Song of Songs: a collection of love-songs (or an elaborate poem) celebrating the love of a man and a woman—surely the most gracious of the many gracious gifts of God to humankind (cf. Gen 1:31).

After a wedding celebration (ch. 9) the story of Tobit hastens to its close. The elderly Tobit meets his son again and is cured of his blindness (11:9-14). And he warmly welcomes his new daughter-in-law (11:17). The book extols family virtues. The older couple, exemplary in their lives, have brought up their children well. Tobias and Sarah, in their turn, have a lofty ideal of marriage and are keenly aware of their obligations to their parents. Great store is set by generous almsgiving. An atmosphere of faith and trust in God—and joyful thanksgiving—is pervasive. This little romance needs no one to plead its cause.

POSSESSION AND VISION

Biblical hope is firmly linked to land: the land of Israel, the land of Galilee and Judea. The covenant of Yahweh and Israel is about land: about promise and possession and loss of land. Israel lived in the hope of a gift, in enjoyment of gift, and in its loss by treating gift as something that belonged of right. Jesus insisted that the Kingdom is gift, to be received only by one who could receive it gladly as a child does. The gift of God is always held in trust. And failure in trust will always lead to loss.

The prophetic movement—as we have already observed in Third Isaiah—continued into the post-exilic age, represented, for instance, by the Isaian school, by Joel and Zechariah. These prophets looked to the day of the Lord when God would judge the whole earth (Is 24:1-23; 25:6-12; Jl 3; Zech 14). They looked to a future for Israel as God brought his plans to fruition (Is 24:23; 35:30; Zech 9:9-10). 'I will strengthen the house of Judah and I will save the house of Joseph. I will bring them back because I have compassion on them, and they shall be as though I had not rejected them' (Zech 10:6; cf. Jl 4:1). The restoration is the deed of the Lord but it will happen as a political reality and with human instrumentality. It will take shape within the context of the nation's history and the history of the world. It will involve possession of the good land (Zech 9:16-17).

The bleak post-exilic situation gave rise to another and different prophetic perspective: apocalyptic eschatology. Visionaries, thoroughly disillusioned with political structure and institutionalised religion, could find no future in human history. They looked to God alone. This outlook can be discerned in the "apocalypses' of Isaiah (Is 26:12; 35:4). It is emphatically present in Daniel. The apocalyptists had a vision of Yahweh's people restored as a holy community in a glorified Zion. They had abandoned hope that it ever could become reality in and through the political and cultic structures of the nation. Those who exercised control over political and religious structures would, too, have looked to restoration, but they were convinced that it would come within those structures. Again, as before, there is tension and again the contending elements are valid—up to a point. On the one hand there is the vision of a divine order transcending human institutions and holding them under judgment. On the other there is concern with the continued life of the community and with the maintenance of the structures. Both these tendencies had been present in the past and the prophets had been able to integrate vision and realism. In the post-exilic period the delicate balance was no longer sustained and that led to polarisation. For some there was present possession—land, or what would stand for land—that is, political structure, ecclesiastical establishment—to be jealously guarded. Others treasured a lively hope, its realisation urgently awaited. As it turned out it was those who waited in hope who were better conditioned to receive the Kingdom.

It is easy to see the apocalyptists as alarmist, hopelessly unrealistic. They may, instead, be reminding us that only God can bring about a kingdom which is the measure of human desire. Historically, the Christian Churches have striven to be so many things. Too often the Church has done 'as the Gentiles do'. The Church will become Kingdom only in God's way and in God's time.

The
New Testament

JOHN THE BAPTIST—*A Voice in the Wilderness*

The gospel portraits of John the Baptist reflect the particular interests of each evangelist. In Mark the Baptist is on the scene at once (Mk 1:2-8) and solemnly proclaims the greater than he. In the Fourth Gospel the Baptist goes out of his way to stress that he is nothing more than a witness to the Light (Jn 1:6-8). Matthew and Luke offer a fuller treatment of the Baptist than does Mark and a more positive evaluation of him than John's.

Mark 1:2-8

The arrival of the Baptist had not been unprepared: he is the messenger (Mal 3:1) and the wilderness prophet (Is 40:3) announced in the scriptures. Clothed like Elijah (2 Kgs 1:8) and subsisting on wilderness fare, John is the sign that in the wilderness God is about to renew his covenant with Israel (Hos 2:14-23; Jer 2:1-30). This mission explains his clarion call to *metanoia*, radical conversion. The response of 'all' Judaea and Jerusalem (Mk 1:8) serves to underline the fact that the divine call to conversion was addressed to the whole of Israel. While John's call to repentance may be seen against the background of a prophetic tradition, his main function is as herald of a greater coming one who will 'baptise with the Holy Spirit'—that is, who will bestow the Spirit.

Mark's account of the death of the Baptist (6:17-29) is dramatic; it is the only narrative in the gospel which is not directly a story about Jesus. And yet it, too, is concerned with him, for it aims to present John as the precursor whose death prefigured the death of Jesus (cf. 9:11-13). The story has been coloured by reminiscences of Old Testament precedents. One can think of Jezebel, who sought Elijah's death (1 Kgs 19:2) for the Baptist, we have noted, was seen as an Elijah figure. Then the influence of the book of Esther is undoubted. This is rather surprising because the characters do not correspond: the wicked Haman and John, the virtuous Esther and Salome have nothing in common. It may well be that in this popular and vivid tale of the Baptist's death reminiscences of Jezebel and Esther are involuntary rather than studied.

The credibility of the Marcan story has been challenged on the ground that it conflicts with Josephus' testimony. According to Josephus, John was imprisoned in the fortress of Machaerus on the east of the Dead Sea and was put to death there. Mark gives the impression that the scene of the banquet (and so of the death of John) was Herod's Galilean capital of Tiberias. Josephus alleges a political motive for John's imprisonment and execution: Herod's fear of a messianic movement sparked by the Baptist's preaching. For Mark the motivation is John's denunciation of Herod's marriage, which aroused the implacable hatred of Herodias. It is noteworthy that the differences between Mark and Josephus centre on the theme of the banquet and the role of Herodias and so stem mostly from the parallelism of the Marcan story with the stories of Jezebel and Esther. And there is the matter of a Herodian princess dancing like a slave-girl. The explanation seems to be that Mark has woven colourful and legendary details into his broadly historical narrative of the fate of the Baptist.

John 1:6-34
More firmly than Mark, the fourth evangelist casts the Baptist in the role of witness and stresses his subordination to the Coming One (1:15). Explicitly, he is *not* the Messiah, *not* Elijah come back to earth, *not* the prophet-like-Moses—traditionally read into Dt 18:15, 18 (Jn 1:19-23). He is a voice, but a heraldic voice. He is one who points out the Lamb of God (1:29, 36), one who has seen the Spirit descend and abide on him who will baptise with Holy Spirit (1:30-33). He is one who declares: 'I have seen and borne witness that this is the Elect of God' (1:34). The fourth evangelist is not seeking directly to downgrade the Baptist; he is indulging in effective polemic against contemporary disciples of the Baptist. The Baptist movement did not end with the death of John. Those who clung to the memory of their Master (Acts 19:1-7 tells of Paul's encounter with such disciples in Ephesus) would have regarded John as a messianic figure. Cleverly, the evangelist has the Baptist emphatically deny that he is Messiah, has him declare himself friend of the bridegroom (3:25-29). He bows from the stage with the gracious words: 'He must increase, but I must decrease' (3:30).

Matthew 3:1-12

Matthew introduces the mission of John the Baptist, herald of the Messiah, with the vague time-reference, 'in those days'. Our interest is straightway caught by a summary of the Baptist's message: (1) Repent, that is, change your attitude; (2) the Kingdom is very near. Crowds come to him for baptism but what matters is the fruit of baptism: they must abandon their false religious securities. The important thing is not an illusory sonship granted by blood or soil but a grace that can be renewed or lost (3:8-9).

The grim warning of verses 7-10 is addressed to 'the Pharisees and Sadducees'. As we know from the gospels and Acts, and from Jewish sources, this is an unlikely alliance. The Baptist is not sanguine that he can make an impression on these professionally religious types. We need to look to the *evangelist's* purpose. For Matthew, John has become the preacher of repentance to Matthew's community. The 'Pharisees and Sadducees' are Christians: John's admonition is addressed to *Christian* leaders. They, too, are in danger of becoming professionally religious. Then no preacher, not even another Baptist, can make any impression on them. They think themselves grain; they may end up as chaff.

Luke

Already in his infancy gospel (Lk 1-2), Luke proleptically characterises the Baptist yet to be born as an ascetic prophet calling Israel to repentance (1:15-17). At his birth an excited rumour ran throughout Judaea: 'What then will this child be?' (1:66). He will be a prophet of the Most High proclaiming the ways of the Lord, pointing the path to forgiveness of sin and salvation (1:76-7).

In 3:7-17 Luke gives samples of the preaching of John the Baptist. Verses 7-9 stress the uncompromising style of his prophetic message; verses 15-18 might be termed his messianic preaching. These are quite the same as Matthew, but the passage 3:10-14 is peculiar to Luke:

> And the multitude asked him, 'What then shall we do?'
> And he answered them, 'He who has two coats, let him share with him who has none; and he who has food, let

him do likewise'. Tax collectors also came to be baptized and said to him, 'Teacher, what shall we do?' And he said to them, 'Collect no more than is appointed you.' Soldiers also asked him, 'And we, what shall we do?' And he said to them, 'rob no one by violence or by false accusation, and be content with your wages.'

For one familiar with the third gospel it is not in the least surprising that the Lucan Baptist should preach in this manner. Among the evangelists, Luke takes a distinctive stance in face of material possessions. His insertion of a 'social' dimension into the Baptist's message is a clever ploy. The precursor strikes a note that will be caught up by the Lord.

The 'multitudes', people in general, are encouraged to share, and share generously, with those in need. One is reminded of Luke's idealised picture of the first Jerusalem community (Acts 2:44-45; 4:33-35): because they shared, 'there was not a needy person among them' (4:34). The message of Jesus will be 'good news to the poor'—'poor' being a blanket term embracing need of every kind, gathering in the marginalised and the rejected. Typical outsiders, tax-collectors (collaborators with Rome) and soldiers (upholders of foreign domination) come to the Baptist and are not repulsed. They are called upon to be honest. They are bidden not to take advantage of military clout which might terrorise, or which might be used to engineer confiscation of property. The Baptist calls for orthopraxis. Doubtless, Luke has Christian readers in view. The Baptist had urged the multitude to 'bear fruits that befit repentance' (3:8); here, in 3:11-14, are examples of 'good fruit'. The Lucan Baptist is laying a foundation for the radical demands of the Lucan Jesus.

Luke 7:18-23 (Mt 11:2-6)

John himself was a prophet of doom who warned that the axe was laid to the root of the trees and, hence, 'every tree that does not bear good fruit will be cut down and thrown into the fire' (Lk 3:9). Furthermore, he is convinced that the Coming One will follow his line: 'his winnowing fork is in his hand ... the chaff he will burn with unquenchable fire' (3:17). In point of fact, Jesus proclaimed that 'the kingdom of God is at hand' (Mk 1:15). Where John prophesied the judgment of God, Jesus prophesied the salvation of God. Hearing, in prison, of the activity of Jesus, a perplexed John sent two of his disciples to enquire: 'Are you he who is to come, or shall we look for another?' (Lk 7:19). And the answer was: 'Go and tell John what you have seen and heard: the blind receive their sight, the lame walk, the poor have the good news preached to them' (7:22). The answer is that while Jesus does not fit the unsparing role the Baptist envisaged, he is attuned to another prophetical tradition. Jesus reminds John (through John's disciples) that he had not come to condemn but to save and that healing, forgiveness and redemption are the hallmark of God's judgment. John is a prophet of doom, in the line of Amos, Jesus a prophet of love and forgiveness, spokesman of the Spouse and Father (Mother) in the manner of Hosea (cf. Hos 1-3; 11).

Luke 7:24-15 (Mt 11:7-19)

How does one evaluate the Baptist? One is not likely to improve on Jesus' assessment of him. Jesus' testimony firmly relates John to God's plan of salvation. The rhetorical questions ('What did you go out into the wilderness to behold?', 7:24, 25, 26) serve to define—in terms of what John was not—the role of the Baptist. John is no reed bending to every breeze but a granite figure; he is no flaccid courtier but a prisoner of conscience in Herod's dungeon. He is indeed a prophet, a spokesman of God. For that matter he is 'more than a prophet' because as *Elijah redivivus* (v. 27) he is precursor of Jesus and because no other, not even one of the prophets of old, is greater than he. The future statement—'yet he who is least in the kingdom of God is greater than he' (v. 28)—does not cancel the unique status of John. Rather, the contrast is between the age of promise and the age of fulfilment. It is quite like Hebrews 11. Following on a eulogy of the faith of the saints of Israel we read: 'And all these, though well attested by their faith, did not receive what was promised' (11:39). The Baptist is great, no doubt of that. But he who is even greater has a vision and a message that transcend the Baptist's.

The role of prophet is never easy. The career of Jeremiah proves that abundantly. And Luke has Jeremiah in mind when announcing the birth of the Baptist. 'He will be filled with the Holy Spirit even from his mother's womb' (Lk 1:15) echoes 'Before I formed you in the womb I knew you...I appointed you a prophet' (Jer 1:5). Jeremiah barely escaped death, more than once; John was put to death. His glory will always be the accolade of the Lord: 'I tell you, among those born of women none is greater than John' (Lk 7:28). Yet, the fact remains, Jesus did not walk the path of the Baptist. John was a prophet of doom. Jesus was a prophet of God's foolish love. Surely, not only in our day but in all days, we need the message of Jesus more than that of John.

John the Baptist was the one who prepared the way of the Lord. His task was 'to turn many...to the Lord their God' (Lk 1:16). It was his task, and he performed well. There is still need for his voice. It is nevertheless sad that in Christian tradition the hell-fire preaching of the Baptist had tended to prevail. The institutional Church has, too often, found the Baptist more congenial than his Lord. The Baptist, true to his conviction, spoke out with courage and paid the price: he had challenged corruption in high places (3:19-20). Jesus had challenged the religious establishment—and paid the price (11:37-54). Baptist and Jesus assure us that we will always need our prophets.

Despite their differences, Jesus and John walked a prophetic way; they shared a pilgrimage that ended in death. Violent death was the seal of authenticity on the integrity of their pilgrim way. The violent death of such as they underlines the obscenity of violence.

MARY OF NAZARETH—*Handmaid of the Lord*

It is a truism that Mary, the mother of Jesus, has played and continues to play, a major role in Christian tradition. While this is so, a first fact that faces any perceptive reader of Scripture is that she is not prominent there. My concern, here, is with the biblical Mary. I am not being a 'minimalist'. I simply look at the texts and present what I find there.

A Negative Old Testament

Two Old Testament texts, Genesis 3:15 and Isaiah 7:14, have become mariologically significant in Christian tradition. Ironically so, because modern scholarship has shown that both texts are incapable of sustaining the mariological assertions made in respect of them.

Gen 3:15

> I will put enmity between you and the woman, and between your seed and her seed; he shall bruise your head, and you shall bruise his heel.

This is word of Yahweh after 'the Fall', a sentence on the cunning snake. For this is what the *nahash* is ('more cunning than any other wild creature that the Lord God had made', 3:1)—a talking-snake playing its role in the story of 3:1-7. In verse 15 we have a typical aetiology—a popular explanation of a phenomenon. Here it accounts for the natural antipathy of humans to snakes. It is war to the death. One stamps on the head of a snake, but the snake may get its strike in first. Significantly, there is no Jewish 'messianic' interpretation of Genesis 3:15. In Christianity only some of the early Fathers interpreted the passage christologically. Irenaeus was one who did so, mistakenly influenced by the *autos* of the Septuagint. The fact is, if the Septuagint has the masculine pronoun *autos*, 'he', following on the neuter *sperma* 'seed', this does not imply a messianic interpretation but an awareness that human 'seed' is in question. The Latin *ipsa*, 'she', of the Vulgate—the obvious basis of mariological interpretation—does not seem to have come from St Jerome himself and reflects a later tradition.

There is no ground at all for that 'she'. The Genesis text does not sustain a mariological interpretation. An exegete has to maintain that Genesis 3:15 is not a *Protoevangelium.*

The other text (Is 7:10-14) need not detain us—it has been looked at earlier.[7] The 'young woman' of 7:14 is the mother of Hezekiah. Matthew, reading the 'virgin' of the Greek text, applied the passage to Mary's motherhood of Jesus (Mt 1:22-23). But it is wrong-headed to read back Matthew's use of the passage into Isaiah's perception of it. As a footnote I would now disagree with colleagues who discern 'daughter of Zion' imagery behind Luke's infancy gospel. And I cannot accept the validity of the patristic 'new Eve' parallel. My own view, as an exegete, is clear: I recognise no Old Testament basis for traditional mariology.

A Gospel Embarrassment

The passage Mark 3:20-35 illustrates the statement in the prologue of the Fourth Gospel: 'He came to his own home, and his own people received him not.' The Marcan section is made up of three passages (the fears of the family of Jesus, vv. 20-21; on collusion with Satan, vv. 20-30; and the true kindred of Jesus, vv. 31-5). It is a typical Marcan 'sandwich' arrangement and so is intended to be read as a unit; the tone is decidedly hostile throughout. The brief narrative of 3:20-21—'then he went home; and the crowds came together again, so that they could not even eat. And when his family heard it, they went out to seize him, for they said, "He is beside himself!"'—has no parallel in Matthew or Luke. The family, concerned for Jesus, had decided to intervene; they fear that he must be out of his mind. Their decision shows a lack of sympathy with his aims and conduct. Independently the Johannine tradition stands in support: 'For even his brothers did not believe in him' (Jn 7:5). The pronouncement-story, Mark 3:31-35, preserves the saying of Jesus that his true kindred are those who do the will of God. Mark's insertion of the Beelzebul/Satan discourse (vv. 22-30) establishes a relationship between the attitude of the family of Jesus, here 'his mother and his brothers', and the attitude of the religious authorities—his own did not receive him. The rhetorical question ('Who are my mother and my brothers?') and reply of

Jesus form the climax of the pronouncement story. There is a marked tone of disappointment in the question; the family of Nazareth have shown that they do not understand him (v. 21).

However embarrassing it may seem to Marian piety, the mother of Jesus stands here with the family as one who did not understand Jesus. Only total refusal to recognise Mark's established 'sandwich' technique can avoid that conclusion. It is significant that Matthew and Luke omit Mark 3:21; and they do contrive to present Mary in a more positive light (Mt 12:46-50; Lk 8:19-21). There is also, of course, Mark 6:3—'Is not this the carpenter, the son of Mary and brother of James and Joses and Judas and Simon, and are not his sisters here with us?' It has to be acknowledged that the *text* of Mark suggests that those brothers and sisters are Jesus' siblings. If 'brothers and sisters' is taken in the broader sense of 'cousins', that is on the basis of factors outside of Mark. Our earliest gospel, then, offers no support at all for a theological assessment of Mary—for mariology.

Luke's Infancy Gospel

The purpose of the infancy gospels (Mt 1-2; Lk 1-2) is firmly christological. There is, however, a mariological intent. Not so much in Matthew's story, let it be said. Yet, even in Matthew, Mary has a not insignificant role. In Luke, Joseph is a stylised figure and Mary is, literally, the *prima donna*. In this short section, I will look to the key passage, the annunciation narrative, Lk 1:26-38. Firstly though, a word about the infancy gospels in general.

Both narratives are quite independent of each other. The common story has Joseph, of Davidic descent, betrothed to Mary. Both evangelists agree on the virginal conception of Jesus and on a heavenly intimation of his name. Jesus was born, after Mary and Joseph had come to live together, in Bethlehem; the child was raised at Nazareth. So far so good; but we are left with many questions. Was Jesus born in Bethlehem because Joseph and Mary lived there (Matthew), or because they had journeyed from Nazareth (Luke)? Did a heavenly choir acclaim his birth (Luke)? Was he acknowledged by Judean shepherds (Luke) or by gentile 'magi' (Matthew)? Many questions, but of no great importance—that is, if we put the proper question to each story: 'What does it mean?' Beyond the basic facts there is little that is strictly historical in the infancy gospels. The two narratives are vehicles of the evangelists' theology and ought to be assessed accordingly.

Luke 1:26-38

Luke asserts the basic fact that Mary was called, and knew herself to be called, to be mother of the Messiah. It was, for her, a profound spiritual experience, a matter between herself and her God, something that took place in the depth of her being. In seeking to give expression to this personal, spiritual experience, Luke spontaneously turned to the Scriptures. He brings before us the angelic messenger: Gabriel, one of the 'angels of the face' of Jewish tradition, who stand in the immediate presence of God; and he provides the dialogue that brings out the significance of the call.

The structure of 1:26-38, like that of 1:5-25 (annunciation of the birth of the Baptist) follows faithfully the Old Testament pattern of angelic annunciations of birth. Hence, material not explained by the literary pattern is significant: the peculiar manner of conception (virginal), the future accomplishments of the child (vv. 32-3, 35) and the portrait of Mary in vv. 34 and 38. 'Hail, O favoured one!'—the opening words of Gabriel are greeting, but scarcely conventional greeting. What is implied is that Mary has been chosen for a unique role in God's plan; she is the object of God's favour because of what is asked of her. Now, too, the statement, 'the Lord is with you', falls into place. Once it is recognised that the title Favoured One is functional, designating a divinely appointed role, then the assurance that the Lord will be with the chosen one is a guarantee of the effective accomplishment of the divine purpose.

Mary is told that she will be mother of a son whom she will name Jesus. In verses 32-3 this Jesus is described as the Davidic Messiah, in terms taken from 2 Sam 7:9-16. Luke uses the technique of Mary's question and Gabriel's answer (vv. 34-5) to point to the true identity of the Davidic Messiah: together they speak Luke's christological message. The Messiah is God's Son and his conception is not by way of marital intercourse (Mary) but through the Holy Spirit (Gabriel). It is Luke's graphic version of an early christological formula, such as that of Romans 1:3-4—'descended from David according to the flesh, and designated Son of God...by his resurrection from the dead'.

Virginal conception of Jesus is proposed both by Matthew and by Luke. It is to be noted that in each of the infancy gospels the second chapter (Mt 2 and Lk 2), read by itself, would not lead to the conclusion of a virginal conception. The question is: how is 'virginal conception' to be understood? There is no echo of this belief elsewhere in the New Testament but it later became widely accepted in Christian belief. One must endorse the need, in our day, of honestly seeking to grasp what the credal formula *natus ex Maria virgine* really intends to say. Is it a *theologoumenon*, a theological statement—or does it necessarily demand biological virginity? What is not in doubt is that both Matthew and Luke are primarily interested in virginal conception as the expression of a christological insight that Jesus was God's son in a unique sense.

On the basis of Mary's question in verse 34—'How can this be, since I have no husband?'—some have asserted that Mary had made a vow of virginity or, at least, had come to understand that she was to remain a virgin. Such speculation is pointless: the question is not a question put by Mary; it is a clever literary device of Luke. In the same vein, from verse 38 we can deduce nothing of Mary's understanding of what was being asked of her. The portrait of her there is shaped from Luke's account of her in the ministry (8:19-21); as one who hears and does the will of God she is truly 'handmaid of the Lord'.

Luke 2:1-21

In the reaction (2:15-20) to birth and heavenly proclamation, the shepherds are forerunners of future believers who will glorify God for what they have heard and will praise God for what they have seen. Here all the protagonists—Mary, Joseph, baby and the shepherds—come together. Yet, only one figure constitutes a bridge from the infancy narrative to the ministry of Jesus and that is Mary his mother. She is that bridge by being a believer and a disciple (Lk 8:19-21; 11:27-18; Acts 1:12-14). This is what Luke intends by his declaration: Mary 'kept all these things, pondering them in her heart' (2:19). One should look to the parallel assertion in 1:51—'his mother kept all these things in her heart'. She, like the Twelve, will come to understanding when Jesus will have risen from the dead. Until then, in the obscurity of faith, she ponders those puzzling events. It is a misunderstanding of Luke's purpose and of his literary achievement, to claim, as some have argued, that these statements point to Mary as source of the evangelist's narrative. Luke had access to some tradition but the infancy gospel, as we have it, is his creation.

The Mary of Luke is a real, warm, thoroughly human person. She was faced with challenge, with decision. What young girl would not be taken aback by the assertion that *God* wished her to be an unmarried mother! If Abraham is man of faith, Mary is surely woman of faith. As Abraham spoke his 'yes', Mary spoke her *fiat*. As Abraham 'went out, not knowing where he was to go' (Heb 11:8), Mary, with her 'let it be done to me according to your word' also handed God an open cheque. For Abraham 'faith was reckoned to him as righteousness' (Rom 4)—the way, the only way, of standing right with God is by saying *yes*, is to let God be God *in his way*. Mary was one who said her 'yes' to God.

The Fourth Gospel

Mary appears twice only in the Fourth Gospel: at Cana and at the foot of the cross. John is a gospel shot through with symbolism. There is no doubt that our passages—2:1-12 and 19:25-7—are symbolic in the extreme. It is very difficult indeed to figure out just what the evangelist had in mind; we must be circumspect in interpretation. The mother of Jesus figures in both scenes, scenes which are connected in the intention of the evangelist. Here is an attempt to discern the role of Mary in these Johannine texts.

John 2:1-12

The Cana episode is theologically important for John. This is made abundantly clear in verse 11—'This, the first of his signs, Jesus did at Cana in Galilee, and manifested his glory, and his disciples believed in him.' 'Signs', 'glory', 'believed'—when we add in 'my hour' (v.4) we have a piling of Johannine theological terms. There is the perennial puzzle of verses 3-5: 'The mother of Jesus said to him, "They have no wine", and Jesus said to her, "O woman, what have you to do with me? my hour has not yet come." His mother said to the servants, "Do whatever he tells you."'" As an exegete I confess myself defeated. Some proposed solutions can be ruled out at once. A rather common one is that, at the request of his mother, Jesus had anticipated the 'hour'. The truth is, in Johannine thought, the 'hour' (the 'glorification': death, resurrection, return to the Father) is solely in the Father's power; not even Jesus can anticipate it. It has to be admitted that it is far from easy to come to terms with the implied request of Mary, the explicit refusal of Jesus, and the further instructions of Mary as though she had not listened to the words of her son. On the level of normal family life such inconsistency is easily accommodated. The snag is that, for the evangelist, the scene is intensely theological. I subscribe to the view of the Johannine scholar, Rudolf Schnackenburg:

> In the two scenes where Mary the mother of the Lord appears, first at the beginning of Jesus' ministry and then at the end, under the cross (19:26-27), does the Evangelist here intend to make deeper 'Mariological' statements or at least provide the basis for them? Here one should aim at soberness and circumspection, even though it seems to be a 'minimizing' exegesis. But if we wish to avoid the errors of the past, the exegete intent on the literal sense will prefer to wring 'too little' than 'too much' out of the text.'[8]

John 19:25-7

> Standing by the cross of Jesus were his mother, and his mother's sister, Mary the mother of Cleopas, and Mary Magdalene. When Jesus saw his mother, and the disciple whom he loved standing near, he said to his mother, 'Woman, behold your son!' Then he said to the disciple, 'Behold your mother!'. And from that hour the disciple took her to his home.

This is a thoroughly symbolic scene. None of the synoptists suggests that the mother of Jesus was present at his execution. Mark lists women, not including Mary, 'looking on from afar'

107

(Mk 15:40). The Beloved Disciple is very important in the Johannine tradition: a disciple of Jesus who was, clearly, the *guru* of the Johannine community. In typical Johannine fashion this prestigious person and the Mother play symbolic roles. Yet again, it is extremely difficult to winkle out what the evangelist really had in mind. One thing is sure: John has no intention of presenting a mater dolorosa. His intent, as at Cana, was to present Mary as the representative of all those who seek true salvation. We should note that if Jesus' mother is handed over to the disciple, the disciple is entrusted to Mary as mother. It is a message for John's community (represented by the Beloved Disciple), a message that the one seeking salvation is to be adopted and cared for.[9]

In my view, the Johannine mariological witness is so obscure as to be unhelpful. It cannot be denied that in his symbolic scenes at Cana and at the Cross, Mary does play a role. But what that role is, is far from clear. One has only to look to the history of exegesis of the Fourth Gospel to get a confused picture. I may end more positively by returning to Luke.

The Woman for Others (Lk 1:39-56; [Jn 2:1-5])

In the structure of the Lucan infancy narrative the 'Visitation' passage is a complementary episode, a pendant to the diptych of annunciations (1:1-38). Elizabeth is granted the perception not only that Mary is with child but that her child is the Messiah. Her canticle in praise of Mary (1:42-5) echoes Old Testament motifs and anticipates motifs that will be found in the body of the gospel (11:27-8). The narrative serves as a hinge between the two birth stories, of John and of Jesus. And this meeting of women illustrates their respective situations. Elizabeth's pregnancy was not only a sign for Mary; it was also an invitation: the 'haste' of Mary was inspired by friendship and caring.

At Mary's greeting Elizabeth felt the infant stir within her—John, while still in the womb, is precursor (1:17) of the Lord. Enlightened by the prophetic Spirit she concluded that Mary is to be the mother of 'the Lord'. That is why Mary is 'blessed among women'—the most blessed of women. Elizabeth went on to praise Mary's acquiescence in God's plan for her—her great faith: 'And blessed is she who believed...'.

Elizabeth had singled out Mary's faith for special attention and she had done so rightly. Still, there remains the more mundane, but refreshingly human, factor that Mary had travelled from Nazareth to Judaea to share the joy of her aged cousin and to lend a helping hand. One may allude to the Cana episode (Jn 2:1-15). True, it is a passage heavy with Johannine theology, but what matters here is that John has cast Mary as a caring and practical woman who could be counted on to supervise, quietly and effectively, a rural wedding. Each in his way, Luke and John have presented her as the woman for others. And this is not a surprise casting of her who is mother of 'the man for others'.

The Suffering Mother (Lk 2:22-35; [Jn 19:25-27])

Luke's real concern in this 'presentation' episode is the witness of Simeon and Anna. Simeon's *Nunc Dimittis* introduces the theme of salvation for the Gentiles. Mary and Joseph were astonished at the glowing prophetic words. In the second oracle (2:34-35) Simeon anticipates the rejection of Jesus by the Jewish authorities and the rejection of the Christian mission to Israel described in Acts. Here is where the mother is drawn into the destiny of her Son. He will be a 'sign of contradiction', a challenge; the thoughts of those hostile to Jesus will come to light.

Mary stands among the smaller group of those who will 'rise' rather than among those who will 'fall'. She, a daughter of Israel, will be tested like the rest. She cannot be different from her son, the one who 'in every respect has been tempted as we are' (Heb 4:15). Mary, too, will be tested and, like him, prove faithful. One recalls John's scene of Mary at the foot of the cross (Jn 19:25-7). His intent was not alone to show Mary as representative of those who seek true salvation but, too, to make the point that those who seek true salvation will meet with suffering. If the Son of Mary 'learned obedience through what he suffered' (Heb 5:8), the mother, too, grew through what she endured. If John has Mary at the foot of the cross, another purpose of that is to suggest that she had, in the light of the resurrection, come to understand the meaning of the cross. Like Paul, she had come to see that the cross is God's definition of God and of humankind. The handmaid of the

Lord, with her openness to God, could grasp the true meaning of the death of her son. Her 'pondering' had come to fruition.

The Real Mary

This picture of a level-headed, practical Mary is a necessary corrective to a widely propagated image of her. Her declaration, 'I am the handmaid of the Lord' has, through misunderstanding, not been helpful to the place of women in the Church. It has been used to maintain them in a wholly passive role: how dare any woman aspire to anything more than Mary!

It seems to me that Elizabeth's beatitude pinpoints what is most significantly helpful about Mary: 'Blessed is she who believed' (Lk 1:45). She is the woman of faith. Popular piety has endowed her with extraordinary gifts. 'Full of grace'—a mistranslation of a Greek word meaning 'favoured one'—gave *carte blanche*. It was assumed that she had been fully enlightened from the first as to the nature and destiny of her Son. So endowed was she thought to have been that she was scarcely human any more. None of this is sustained by the gospel texts. In the gospels she appears very much one of us, as indeed she is. If her Son is like us in all things, the same must surely be true of the Mother. Nor does Mary's sinlessness make her any less human. Sin, whatever form it may take, detracts from our full humanness. Mary, as one wholly free of sin, was wholly human. And being human necessarily involves the limitations of humanness. Sinlessness does not imply superhuman endowment, does not make one immune to suffering and to death.

There is one other point: Mary's Magnificat (Lk 1:46-55—which figures prominently in the Liberation theology of Latin America. It is noteworthy that a woman, addressing a woman, emphasises God's preferential option for the poor. This woman speaks a subversive message. The traditional subservience of Mary must be challenged. The gospel Mary is no passive figure. It is by acknowledging her whole and wholesome womanhood that she can be set free to further the cause of her sisters—not to be used against them.

While John the Baptist belonged essentially to the past, Mary was a link between the Old and the New. She had lived, to the full, her Jewish faith, she, a model of the *anawim*. Her

110

spiritual pilgrimage led her to the light of resurrection-faith.
As far as we know, her life was lived in the quiet of Nazareth.
Yet, there were journeys: to 'a city of Judah', with return to
Nazareth; then, soon after, to Bethlehem and back. There were
pilgrim journeys to Jerusalem. And there was the journey to
the Cross. Mary's whole life was a journey to 'the city which is
to come' (Heb 13:14).

MARY MAGDALENE—*Apostle to the Apostles*

Until quite recently it was simply assumed that the term
'disciple', in the New Testament, meant a *male* disciple. Today
we are more aware that the assumption flowed from an androcentric (male-centred) reading of an androcentric text: double
myopia. The truth, we now realise, is that women had, some-
how, slipped into that androcentric text. Admittedly, they are
thin on the ground—but they are there! Typically, it is the
plain, blunt Mark who gives the game away:

> There were also women looking on from afar, among
> whom were Mary Magdalene, and Mary the mother of
> James the younger and of Joses, and Salome, who, when
> he was in Galilee, followed him, and ministered to him;
> and also many other women who came up with him to
> Jerusalem (Mk 15:40-41).

Here—the occasion is the crucifixion of Jesus—Mark acknowledges the scandalous reality of women disciples; Matthew and
Luke advert to them more discreetly (Mt 27:55-56; Lk
23:55;56). This fact of women disciples is revolutionary. We
must picture not our modern western world where, in theory
at least, women are acknowledged as equal and an easy relationship between men and women is taken for granted. In the first-
century Palestinian world of Jesus' day such free association
was anything but the norm. A mixed discipleship group was
unconventional—scandalous in fact. In the earliest Church,
remembrances of Jesus' precedent was a powerful factor.

111

Unhappily, equality of women quickly proved to be too tall an order. Today, we are better situated to appreciate the challenge of Jesus' call to women. The fact remains that women will have to fight every inch of the way towards equality. That road to justice is the specific pilgrimage of women. They might find inspiration and hope in Mary Magdalene—a Mary rescued from an unfortunate and unkind rating of her.

Tradition has been cruel to Mary Magdalene. The characterisation of her as a reformed prostitute has gone almost unchallenged. The truth is: there is not a shred of evidence to sustain that estimation of her. A factor is that she emerges for the first time in Luke's gospel immediately after his story of 'the woman in the city who was a sinner' (Lk 7:36-50). Whether or not his anonymous woman was a prostitute ('sinner' is a vague term) has nothing to do with the subsequent reference to 'Mary, called Magdalene, from whom seven demons had gone out' (8:2). Traditionally, the 'seven demons' have been taken to imply sexual immorality and Mary has been identified with that woman of chapter 7 (who was regarded as a prostitute). From parallel texts, for example the Gerasene demoniac passage (5:1-20), it is clear that possession by 'seven demons' means that Mary had been a mentally ill woman, healed by Jesus. To class her as 'sinner' is calumny. It seems to me that the Christian rehabilitation of Mary Magdalene is long overdue. One is not suggesting that a onetime sinner might not become a follower of Jesus and a saint. But there is no excuse for classifying Mary as a reformed prostitute. The presentation of her in the synoptic—and more so in the Johannine—traditions is thoroughly positive.

Luke 8:1-3; Mark 15:40-41; 16:1-8

Luke names Mary Magdalene for the first time as one of a group of women (Lk 8:1-3). Some of them had been healed by Jesus of 'evil spirits and diseases'; Mary, 'from whom seven demons had gone out', had been healed of a severe mental illness. It is true that Luke speaks of these Galilean women only as 'providing for them (Jesus and the twelve) out of their means'; he refrains from explicitly designating them disciples as Mark had done. Still, even he acknowledges that Jesus was unconventional in having women among his group.

Mark (15:40-41), earlier than Luke, is more forthcoming. The women who, standing at a distance, witnessed the crucifixion of Jesus, are said to be those who 'followed him'—a technical term for discipleship. For that matter, the 'many other women' mentioned in the same context are also disciples. They were Galileans who had 'come up with him' to Jerusalem—again discipleship. It was because they had continued to follow him to the cross, if only 'from afar', that the final message was entrusted to them: 'Go, tell his disciples and Peter that he is going before you to Galilee' (16:7). They alone had followed to the cross. The chosen men disciples, the inner circle, had abandoned Jesus. These women disciples had stood steadfast and had not been ashamed of Jesus (cf. 8:38).

The Fourth Gospel

The fourth evangelist has heightened the effect by concentrating the women-witness in the dramatic figure of Mary Magdalene. In the first place, he had Mary Magdalene, in the symbolic scene of 19:25-7, standing *by* the cross of Jesus. But it is in 20:1-18 that she comes into her own.

> Now on the first day of the week Mary Magdalene came to the tomb early, while it was still dark, and saw that the stone had been taken away from the tomb. So she ran and went to Simon Peter and the other disciple, and one whom Jesus loved, and said to them, 'They have taken the Lord out of the tomb, and we do not know where they have laid him' (20:1-2).

Underlying this passage would seem to be the earliest form of an empty tomb narrative in any gospel. John has introduced the Beloved Disciple and has, for his own dramatic purpose, reduced the original group of women to Mary Magdalene, preparing the way for the later christophany to her (vv. 14-18). It is this christophany, and not the words of an angelic spokesman (Mk 16:5-7), which solves the riddle of the empty tomb (vv. 12-13). The tradition which John had followed is early indeed.

John 20:11-13, the brief conversation between Mary and the angels, is little more than a rewriting of verse 2—it is necessary to get back to Magdalene after the independent episode of verses 3-10: Peter and the Beloved Disciple at the tomb. A recurring theme of the resurrection narratives is that the Lord is not at once recognised (Lk 24:16, 37; Jn 20:14-15; 21;4); it required some word or familiar gesture of his to make him known. This is an effective way of making the point that Jesus had not returned to life as before but had passed, beyond death, to *new* life with God. He is Jesus—and yet he is different. The appearance stories are heavily laden with theological and apologetic motifs. The most striking example is here—20:14-16. Mary Magdalene, of all people, 'turned round and saw Jesus standing, but she did not know that it was Jesus' (20:14)! More remarkably, she took him to be the gardener and wondered if he were the one who had removed the body of the Lord (v. 15)! Then the dénouement: 'Jesus said to her, "Mary." She turned and said to him in Hebrew, "Rabboni"' (v. 16).

The brief dialogue is theologically rich. Jesus is the one who had sought out Mary—he is the one 'who calls his own sheep by name' (10:3); Mary is one who 'knows his voice' (v. 4). The Risen One is indeed the Good Shepherd who knows those who belong to him; Mary stands for believers who hear and follow his call. Though the risen one is none other than Jesus, he encounters Mary in a new way: 'Jesus said to her, "Do not hold me, for I have not yet ascended to the Father; but go to my brethren and say to them, I am ascending to my Father and your Father, to my God and your God"' (20:17). The Jesus who speaks is the glorified one; yet, his 'hour' will not be complete until he has breathed the Holy Spirit on his disciples (10:21). In John's view, the 'hour' of Jesus comprises the death, resurrection, return to the Father, installation in glory, return as Paraclete. Human language cannot accommodate all that the 'hour' holds. 'I have not yet ascended' and 'I am ascending' express that limitation.

Mary had been bidden: 'Go to my brethren'—*apostola apostolorum*. And her message was: 'I have seen the Lord' (10:18). After this, there can be no doubting the stature of Mary Magdelene. The story is all the more remarkable because our earliest account of resurrection appearances ascribes the initial appearance to Cephas (1 Cor 15:5). Despite that, the later Johannine picture emphatically gives the honour to Mary

Magdalene. An important strand of gospel tradition proposes a woman as the privileged person who had first met the risen Lord; the assertion is taken up in the 'longer ending' of Mark (16:4). Admittedly, that same tradition specifies that the Beloved Disciple had believed in resurrection even before he had encountered the Lord (20:8). The fact remains that the Johannine Mary stands as a challenge. I suspect that she had been seen as a threatening figure. The traditional casting of her as a reformed prostitute cut her down to size. Rehabilitation of this gospel heroine would notably advance the cause of women. She would be an inspiration and a support in their pilgrimage towards full citizenship in the household of the Lord.

BARNABAS—*Son of Encouragement*

Acts of the Apostles, as second part of Luke's great work Luke-Acts, is more truly a sequel to the gospel than a history of the early Church. The value of Acts lies primarily in Luke's theological reflections on the spread of the Good News—the stages of 'the Way', his distinctive term for the life-style of the Christian community (e.g. Acts 9:2; 24:14). He is not pre-occupied with historical detail—though his story of how things went is broadly right. His purpose was to tell his readers what they should look for and discover: a community called into being by God's Son and guided on its way by God's Spirit.

Attention to the literary dimension of Luke's work is revealing. There is, for instance, the factor of characterisation. In literary terms, 'characters' are not the same as people. In day-to-day life we know one another imperfectly. I may guess at your thoughts; I cannot really know what you are thinking. Characters can be transparent. The narrator may fully expose a character to his reader, can permit the reader to get inside the character. Alternatively, he can present a 'true' picture of any character. The gospels, in which Jesus is a literary character, make him known to us more clearly than he, as a person, was in fact known to his contemporaries. Here we look at a relatively minor character in Acts—one, however, with unusual charm.

Son of Encouragement

When, in Acts, we first encounter Barnabas, we learn of his generosity and recognise in it an example of Luke's community ideal of sharing goods.

> Joseph, who was surnamed by the apostles Barnabas (which means, Son of encouragement), a Levite, a native of Cyprus, sold a field which belonged to him and brought the money and laid it at the apostles' feet (4:36-7).

We shall see that this Joseph was well nicknamed 'the son of encouragement'. As we proceed, I believe it will be clear that here is a man who has a message for all of us.

We next meet Barnabas in connection with Paul:

> And when Paul had come to Jerusalem he attempted to join the disciples; and they were all afraid of him, for they did not believe that he was a disciple. But Barnabas took him and brought him to the apostles, and declared to them how on the road he had seen the Lord (9:26-7).

It is not really surprising that Christians were suspicious of Paul. After all, he was one who had consented to the death of Stephen (8:1). He was one who had 'breathed threats and murder against the disciples of the Lord' (9:1) and had set out for Damascus that he might arrest men and women who followed 'the way'. The intervention of Barnabas was decisive. He was a man who had won the respect of his fellow Christians. He was a man of perception who had discerned the great potential of Paul. His generosity in selling his property and surrendering the proceeds was indicative of his character. He was even more generous in recognising the talents and promise of another. He was not content with recognition and moved to active support. Would Saul have become the great Paul if Barnabas had not sponsored him? In Luke's telling of the story, he would not. Of course, the whole affair was directed by the Holy Spirit. But, in God's plan, the role of Barnabas was a vitally important one.

Our next encounter with Barnabas is in connection with the conversion of Gentiles at Antioch. The Jerusalem Church had

116

been told of this development and had sent Barnabas to investigate. His reaction was positive and enthusiastic:

> When he came and saw the grace of God, he was glad; and
> he exhorted them all to remain faithful to the Lord with
> steadfast purpose (11:23).

Because of opposition in Jerusalem, Paul had had to retire to his home town of Tarsus. But Barnabas had not forgotten the promising Saul. Things were not going well in Antioch. Barnabas felt that here was an area where Saul could make a contribution. 'So Barnbaas went to Tarsus to look for Saul, and when he had found him he brought him to Antioch' (11:25-6). Here, again, is the encouragement and support that even Paul needed. Barnabas's concern was the furthering of the cause of Christ. He was not at all worried about his own contribution and standing. He discerned that Paul had so much to offer—and he backed him to the hilt.

When the Antioch community decided to widen its scope and reach out to the Gentiles, the two chosen for the task were Barnabas and Saul. Very soon (Acts 13-14) Saul (henceforth known as Paul) assumed the leadership. Barnabas quietly went along with this arrangement. He was senior but had always been aware of the calibre of Paul and he permitted Paul to take over.

Paul and Barnabas, returned from this successful mission, were sent as delegates to Jerusalem to plead the cause of the Gentile mission. Though by this stage Paul was the dominant figure we may presume that Barnabas, who was patently a diplomat, would have played no small part in getting the suspicious Jewish Christians to accept this daring venture of openness to the Gentiles (15:1-29). At any rate, the pair could return to Antioch with the satisfaction of knowing that the problem of Gentile converts had been resolved (15:10-35). Christianity would be a religion of humankind—not a Jewish sect. Paul would continue to encounter the bitter opposition of judaisers; but the principle had been established.

Contention

Then occurred an incident which sharply reminds us that Christianity is a religion of real people. In its own way the sad passage 15:36-40 is comforting. Paul had decided that he and Barnabas should embark on another missionary project. That was fine. The snag was that John Mark, Barnabas's cousin (Col 4:10) had backed out of their previous missionary journey (Acts 13:13). Paul will not have Mark. So, what happens? 'There arose a sharp contention so that they separated from each other' (15:39).

There is no suggestion that Paul and Barnabas ever met again, much less that they were reconciled. We do perceive that Barnabas emerged from the sorry affair with more dignity than Paul. What we have hitherto observed of Barnabas shows him to be a magnanimous man. Here he has overlooked the failure of Mark—seemingly a young man, understandably nervous of the ambitious plans of Paul. Barnabas well knew that Paul had no need of him any more. True, it was he who had 'discovered' Paul and had helped and supported him when he needed help. His instinct for Paul's sterling qualities had been proved right. As we have seen, Paul promptly assumed leadership of the mission. Barnabas had not only accepted that situation but would have been content to accompany Paul on another missionary venture. Now it was John Mark who needed help and support. Barnabas faced a decision: Paul or Mark. Characteristically, he chose Mark. It was not an easy choice. He was fond of Paul and this rift must have caused him pain. But, as 'son of encouragement', his course was clear.

Such is Luke's account of the clash between Paul and Barnabas—significantly at Antioch (14:35). Paul himself (Gal 2:11-14) shows us that the occasion of the break was theological controversy. After the Jerusalem decision on the unconditional acceptance of Gentile converts (2:1-10), Peter had gone to Antioch and, at first, had joined in table-fellowship with Gentile Christians. But, on the arrival of others from James's Jewish Christian community, he discontinued the practice. Paul promptly accused him of duplicity. And he adds: 'And with him the rest of the Jews acted insincerely, so that even Barnabas was carried away by their hypocrisy' (2:13). Whatever the reason for the conduct of Peter and Barnabas, Paul regarded this unwillingness on the part of Jewish Christians to have table-fellowship—including eucharistic table-fellowship—with their Gentile brothers and sisters as a practical repudiation of what had been decided in Jerusalem and as a deadly blow to his gospel of union of Jew and Gentile in the faith of Jesus Christ. He could no longer make common cause with Barnabas.

Luke—who now takes leave of Barnabas—did not want the onus for the rift to fall on that magnanimous man. Barnabas steps from the stage, then, without a blot on his character. He stands as a model. In Christian life—as in any community—some will have qualities of initiative and leadership and will, in one area or another, become prominent. This is natural and inevitable. Yet, all the while, on our pilgrim way, there is plenty of scope for the role of Barnabas. His talent would be a valuable asset of a teacher, for instance, or a pastor. To be a Barnabas what is needed, first of all, is faith in the goodness and power of God. What is needed is discernment, an eye for the qualities of others. What is needed is generosity; one rejoices at the success of others. What is needed is the wisdom to know when to bow out. What is needed is—humility. Barnabas is not a major figure for Luke. We cannot doubt that he stands very high in the estimation of the Lord. Very likely we shall get a surprise in due course when, at the close of our pilgrim way, we see, in heaven, the Barnabases of this world get, at last, their deserved recognition. Would it not be nice to find ourselves among them!

PAUL—*Apostle*

The first Christians proclaimed Jesus to be Messiah. For Saul of Tarsus the claim was intolerable. That man, Jesus of Nazareth, had been duly condemned by the sanhedrin—the supreme religious council of the Jews—and had been crucified. The curse of God had fallen upon him: 'Cursed be everyone who hangs on a tree' (Dt 21:23; cf. Gal 3:13). It was perverse and sinful to claim that Jesus was Messiah of Israel. No wonder, then, that Saul 'persecuted the church of God violently and tried to destroy it' (Gal 2:13). That same

Saul—now signing himself 'Paul'—had opened that letter to the Galatians with a clarion challenge:

> I, Paul an apostle—not from men nor through men, but through Jesus Christ and God the Father (Gal 1:1).

There is a pilgrimage indeed! And what a pilgrim! Paul was a Jew, through and through. He had been a thorough-going Pharisee (Phil 3:4-6). He had never had any doubt as to his own identity: 'I myself am an Israelite' (Rom 11:1). The pilgrimage from single-minded persecutor of disciples of the Nazarene to foremost missionary and theologian of Christianity was a unique journey. It can be sketched here only with the broadest strokes.

The first point to be made is that this surely was not a journey *from* Judaism. Paul is never shy about putting forward his own views; on this point he is eloquent. He writes of other Jewish Christians with whom he had serious theological differences. They had alleged that he was no longer a real Jew. His response is categorical:

> If any other man thinks he has reason for confidence in the flesh, I have more: circumcised on the eighth day, of the people of Israel, of the tribe of Benjamin, a Hebrew born of Hebrews, as to the law a Pharisee, as to zeal a persecutor of the church, as to righteousness under the law blameless (Phil 3:4-6).

There is no hiding the pride that shines through these words: Paul is *proud* to be a Jew. That is why, when Paul goes on—'Whatever gain I had, I counted as loss for the sake of Christ' (3:7)—he is not at all apologising for his conviction and conduct of the past. He is saying that he now views the past in a new light.

Never, for a moment, would Paul contemplate any betrayal of his Jewishness. He had come to believe, with passionate conviction, that in Jesus he had found the Messiah, the goal of Jewish expectation. One may well find that chapters 9-11 of Romans do not represent the easiest and clearest part of Paul's writings. But one cannot fail to be moved by the feeling that pervades these chapters. Paul will simply *not* accept that God had rejected his people: 'They are Israelites, and to them

120

belong the sonship, the glory, the covenants, the giving of the law, the worship, and the promises; to them belong the patriarchs, and of their race, according to the flesh, is the Christ' (9:4-5). His argumentation is tortuous, simply because the problem he addresses is so puzzling: how could God's people have failed to recognise God's Messenger? Paul had never lost sight of his conviction that 'the gifts and the call of God are irrevocable' (11:29). In the light of that conviction he can declare: 'and so all Israel will be saved' (11:26).

In 2 Corinthians Paul vehemently defends his apostleship against opponents of his: Christian missionaries of Jewish origin. They, evidently, had stressed their Jewishness, they were Hebrews, Israelites, descendants of Abraham. Paul makes equal claims: 'Are they Hebrews? So am I. Are they Israelites? So am I. Are they descendants of Abraham? So am I' (11:22).

One needs to be careful about how one thinks of the 'conversion' of Paul. It should not be regarded as a crossing over from one religion to another; the Christian movement did not become a religion distinct from Judaism until after the time of Paul. Above all, in no way at all had he repudiated his Jewishness. If he did come to take a stand against the absolute claim of Torah (Gal 3:23-25) that did not mean rejection of the Hebrew Scriptures.

For Freedom

There is no doubt that when he wrote Galatians Paul was an angry man. This is clear from the very tone of the letter. The judaisers (Christians with a background of pharisaic Judaism) who were, successfully it appears, persuading the Galatians to take on board observance of the Mosaic law, evoked memories that still rankled of former opponents of his in Antioch—those 'false brethren secretly brought in, who slipped in to spy out our freedom which we have in Christ Jesus, that they might bring us into bondage' (Gal 2:4). At a meeting in Jerusalem (Gal 2; Acts 15) Paul's view won the day: one could be a Christian without becoming a Jew—a crucial decision for the future of Christianity. The 'pharisee party' had been defeated. But this upset did not signal the end of them. Paul had to sustain their assaults throughout his ministry.

For all his new vision there remained, in Paul, a tension

121

between his being in Christ and his being a Jew. But he would not resolve that tension by collapsing Jew and Gentile into a third entity. And it is this which explains a certain ambivalence in his attitude to the Law. 'As a Jew he regarded the law as embodying the will of God and its precepts as self-evidently true except when he had cause to renounce them. It is thus natural that when he dealt with behaviour he had recourse to the law. This may have led to logical inconsistencies, but humanly it is quite understandable.'[10] The Church is the 'Israel of God' (Gal 6:16)—a community in which Jewish Christians might retain their attachment to Torah and Temple and in which Gentile Christians might make their way without Torah and Temple. In the 'church of God' Paul looked for freedom, not uniformity. His harsh attitude to 'law'—in Galatians, for instance—was, in part, because legalism brings a stultifying sameness, because it stifles the Spirit. And Christ has called us to freedom, the freedom of the children of God (Gal 5:1; Rom 8:21).

Peregrinatio pro Christo

I have outlined what might be termed a pilgrimage of the spirit. The pilgrimage of Paul the missionary was, literally, a journey of sweat and blood. Paul was the first great *peregrinus pro Christo*—as the Irish missionary monks liked to call themselves. We have to figure out the direction and path of his journey. The traditional 'three missionary journeys' come from our reading of the text of Acts rather than from any clear assertion of Luke. While Luke does point us along the footsteps of Paul, his presentation of Paul's travels is dictated by his own theological concern. For him the ultimate goal of Paul's missionary achievement was Rome. He makes this point in the programmatic statement: 'You shall be my witnesses in Jerusalem and in all Judaea and Samaria and to the end of the earth' (Acts 1:8). The 'end of the earth' is Rome, capital of the Roman Empire: effectively the 'world' of the New Testament age. That Rome was envisaged as the climax of his worldwide apostolic activity is in flat contradiction of Paul's own design. In the first place, Rome already had a flourishing Christian community; Paul's endeavour was to break new ground (Rom 15:20). Besides, Paul had made his own intention crystal clear:

the Roman visit would be just that. He wanted to meet the Roman Christians, but he would soon be on his way to Spain, speeded, he hoped, by the Roman community (Rom 15:23-24, 28). Paul's goal was not Rome but Spain, the western limit of the Roman world.

Paul's missionary strategy was never haphazard. He set out to found stable Christian communities. And he carefully planned the siting of the communities: in the principal cities of the Empire. He selected cities that would prove natural centres of expansion—especially seaports. Once he had established a Christian community—and this required a longer stay than Luke sometimes allows for—he could move on, convinced that he had left behind a viable missionary centre.

Luke is surely right in naming the important city of Antioch on the Orontes as source of the first mission to the Gentiles, undertaken by Barnabas and Saul (Acts 12:1-2). It seems that after the unhappy confrontation with Peter and Barnabas recorded in Gal 2:11-14, Paul had nothing more to do with Antioch. Henceforth, he would go it alone. His stated policy was: 'to preach the gospel, not where Christ had already been named, lest I build on another man's foundation' (Rom 15:20). This being so, after the Antioch incident, he appears to have assumed that the east was adequately catered for. He turned to the west: 'From Jerusalem and as far round as Illyricum I preached the gospel of Christ' (Rom 15:19). The Pauline stages, then, are significant. Philippi, a Roman colony in north-eastern Macedonia, linked Greece, along the Egnatian Way, with the rest of the western world. Thessalonica, capital of the province of Macedonia, was a busy seaport. Corinth, capital of the province of Achaia (southern Greece) was highly cos-mopolitan, one of the most important cities of the Empire. Ephesus, though not capital of the province of Asia, was a notable seaport and, as home of the temple of Artemis (Diana), was world-famous.

The pattern suggests that Paul's primary targets were sea-ports; from them his gospel of the crucified and risen Christ could flow. The Galatian community is the exception that proves the rule. Paul reminds the Galatians: 'You know it was because of a bodily ailment that I preached the gospel to you at first" (Gal 4:13). While passing through Galatia, illness forced

123

him to call a halt. Never one to miss an opportunity, he availed of the enforced stay to found a community. Paul's was no aimless pilgrimage; it was a carefully planned project. Each of his communities was established in a city from where the good news might readily spread.

The Cost

The personal cost to Paul of his missionary endeavour was enormous. Most painful was the fierce antagonism of some of his Christian brethren. It was just such opposition which wrenched from Paul an impassioned listing of his trials:

> Are they servants of Christ? I am a better one—I am talking like a madman—with far greater labours, far more imprisonments, with countless beatings, and often near death. Five times I have received at the hands of the Jews the forty lashes less one. Three times I have been shipwrecked; a night and a day I have been adrift at sea; on frequent journeys, in danger from rivers, danger from robbers, danger from my own people, danger from Gentiles, danger in the city, danger in the wilderness, danger at sea, danger from false brethren; in toil and hardship, through many a sleepless night, in hunger and thirst, often without food, in cold and exposure. And, apart from other things, there is the daily pressure upon me of my anxiety for all the churches (2 Cor 11:23-28).

An impressive catalogue indeed. Yet, his last trial must have been the most painful of all: the savage frustration of his plans. He had written, confidently, to the Romans:

> I hope to see you in passing as I go to Spain, and to be sped on my journey there by you, once I have enjoyed your company for a little while. At present, however, I am going to Jerusalem with aid for the saints . . . When, therefore, I have completed this, and have delivered to them what has been raised, I shall go on by way of you to Spain (Rom 15:24-5, 28).

No reading between the lines here. Paul is straightforward and clear. Because, for Luke, Paul's goal has to be Rome, there is no reason to question the broad lines of his account of how Paul did get there. Paul's visit to Jerusalem turned out badly. He fell victim of Jewish outrage against an alleged traitor to Judaism. Whisked, for his own safety, to the Caesarea headquarters of the Roman procurator, he languished in prison for two years during the office of Antonius Felix. When the new procurator, Porcius Festus, briefed by the Jewish leaders, wanted him to stand trial in Jerusalem, Paul, as a Roman citizen, appealed to the imperial tribunal. He did reach Rome, but as a prisoner (Acts 21:27–28:16). And there he met his death.

Paul's ambitious plan of a journey to Spain never took shape. He had probably found from experience that his own words were more true than he had realised when he wrote them: 'For the foolishness of God is wiser than men, and the weakness of God is stronger than men' (1 Cor 1:25). Is God, then, a God who toys with his most faithful servants? The stories of Jeremiah and Paul would suggest as much. What is the point of a pilgrimage that ends in failure? The answer is that God is on the side of the losers, not the winners. And, surely, it is more heroic to wend one's way to a goal marked 'Failure' than to stride to the victor's podium. The real question, of course, is: What is success—or failure? The question, fully answered by Jesus, has been well answered by Paul.

MARK—*Pioneer*

One may introduce Mark by asking two questions: (a) Who is Mark? (b) Why did he write a *gospel*? The first question can, at one level, be answered straight off: we do not know. True, the tradition of the early Church is well nigh unanimous in attributing a gospel to 'Mark' who is regularly said to have been the disciple and interpreter of Peter. It has been claimed that he was the 'Mark' or 'John surnamed Mark' mentioned in the New Testament: in Acts, in Philemon, in the deutero-paulines (Colossians, 2 Timothy) and in 1 Peter. There is no compelling reason to believe that this *Markos*—who may not have been the same person throughout since it was a common name—was our evangelist. The answer to the question, at a deeper level, will emerge, as well as the answer to our second question: why did he write a gospel? A study of his work will reveal something of the man and will point to his purpose in writing a gospel.

It is not, I believe, superfluous to state at the outset what I take a gospel to be. Gospel is a new kind of literary form. Jewish and Greek parallels of a sort there may be, but there is nothing quite like it outside the New Testament. The later apocryphal gospels—writings, in great part, of Christian piety—are pale reflections of the real thing. Our gospels are a mixture of narrative and discourse, centred on the person, life and teaching of Jesus of Nazareth, with special emphasis on his death and resurrection. He is the focus; he gives meaning to all. A gospel is not an objective biography—if wholly objective biography is even possible. This story is shot through with resurrection-faith. A gospel is written for believers: it is a Christian document addressed to Christians. More specifically, each of the gospels was, in the first place, written for a certain Christian community and with the needs of that community firmly in mind.

The gospel of Mark has been dated to *c.* AD 65 and is said to have been written in Rome. While Roman provenance, through far from certain, may stand, it becomes increasingly evident that our earliest gospel was written shortly after AD 70. A main argument is that chapter 13 is best understood against the background of the Roman destruction of Jerusalem in AD 70. What eventually matters is the purpose and message of the gospel. Underestimated from early times because of its brevity (almost all of Mark is found in Matthew and Luke), and because of the relatively poor standard of its Greek, in our day Mark has come into its own. In a special way this evangelist stands side by side with Paul as a stalwart proclaimer of a *theologia crucis*—a theology of the cross. And, congenial to modern christology, the Marcan Jesus is the most human of all. Mark has set the pattern of a gospel: it is concerned with christology and discipleship. Jesus is Son of God—God-appointed leader of the new covenant people; he is the 'son of man', the human one who had come to serve, the one faithful unto death. One who has come to terms with the cross (the meaning of his death) can know him and can confess him—as the centurion could and did (15:39). Jesus' disciples did not understand him before Calvary. The Christian reader of the first century and of today is being challenged to come to terms with the love of God manifest in the cross of Jesus.

Happily, there is much in Mark that we can grasp independently of any view on origin and date. This is particularly true of his christological position and of his understanding of discipleship. These are, in the main, so clear that we may suggest another reason for the neglect of this gospel: it is uncompromisingly uncomfortable. Mark's perspective is certainly clear in one predominant aspect: suffering messiahship and suffering discipleship. Mark's Christian faith is firmly anchored in the risen Lord. But he is keenly conscious of living 'between the times'; between the resurrection and the consummation. Victory is the destiny of the faithful Christian. But life in the here and now is real and earnest and can be grim. Mark acknowledges that Christian existence is paradoxical. He finds it normal that it should be so. Jesus won his victory through suffering and death. There is no other way of Christian living nor path to Christian victory. Mark has written that his Christians should understand and accept this. We learn much of Mark himself from his telling of the Jesus-story.

The Authorities
Like most stories, the events and actions of the Marcan story involve conflicts and Jesus is the immediate cause of the conflicts. We may illustrate this factor by glancing, firstly, at the conflicts between Jesus and the authorities and then at those between Jesus and his disciples. The authorities involved are the religious and political leaders—and in relation to them Jesus is at a disadvantage. Mark does indeed show Jesus having facile authority over evil spirits—the exorcisms; and over nature—the stilling of the tempest. But Jesus' authority does not extend to lording it over *people* even though what Jesus says and does directly challenges the authorities in Israel. For their part, the authorities see themselves as defending God's law. They contend that Jesus assumes extensive legal authority for himself, interprets the law in ways they consider illegal, and disregards many religious customs. They respond by making charges against him.

Jesus had been anointed to usher in God's rule (1:9-11); the issue for him was how to get the authorities to 'see' God's authority in his actions and teaching. The narrator carefully created tension and suspense. By the end of the five conflict-stories (2:1—3.6) the sides are clearly established (3:6). The impending clash with the authorities dominates the journey to Jerusalem (8:27–10:52). The climactic confrontation in Jerusalem comes quickly. It is noteworthy that the first accusation against Jesus is the charge of blasphemy: 'Why does this man speak thus? It is blasphemy' (2:7). From the beginning of the story, Jesus walks a tightrope. Nevertheless, the reader sees that Jesus is firmly in control. At the trial he himself volunteers the evidence they need. '"Are you the Christ, the Son of the Blessed?" and Jesus said "I am"' (14:61-2). Jesus, not the authorities, determines his fate.

The narrator resolves the conflict between Jesus and the authorities only when they condemn Jesus and put him to death. It is an ironic resolution: the authorities have co-operated in bringing about God's plan. Through the ironic resolution, the story depicts Jesus as the real authority in Israel. They condemn as blasphemy Jesus' claim to be Son of God but since, in the story world, Jesus' claim is true, *they* are the ones guilty of blasphemy. This irony is, of course, hidden from the authorities, but it is not hidden from the reader. The reader knows that Jesus will be established in power and the authorities condemned (8:28–9:1; 12:24-7, 30-32; 14:62).

The Disciples

At stake in conflict with the disciples is whether Jesus can make them good disciples. The disciples struggle at every point to follow Jesus but are simply overwhelmed by both him and his demands. Jesus' efforts to lead the disciples to understand are matched by their hardness of heart and their fear. Theirs is not that determined opposition to Jesus of the authorities—they are trying to be his followers. Yet, they consistently misunderstand him. In fact, they share the values of the authorities; however, they do follow Jesus to Jerusalem.

Nevertheless, Jesus just cannot lead his chosen disciples to understand him, cannot get them to do what he expects of them. In an effort to bring them to realise how blind and dense they are, he hurls rhetorical questions at them (4:13, 40;

8:17–21, 33; 9:19; 14:37, 41)—and he is met with silence. He tries to prepare them for his impending death and for his absence. He knows that they will fail him in Jerusalem; yet he seeks to urge them to stand by him (14:37, 41-2). The outer conflict reflects an inner conflict within the disciples: they want to be loyal to Jesus but not at the cost of giving up everything, least of all their lives.

Jesus does not manage to make them faithful disciples. They fail him—and the question stands: will they learn from their failure and, beyond his death, become true followers of him? When Jesus warned his followers of their impending failure (14:26-31), he added a reassuring word: 'After I am raised up, I will go before you to Galilee' (14:28). That word is then caught up in the message of the 'young man' at the tomb: 'Go, tell his disciples, and Peter, that he is going before you to Galilee; there you will see him, as I told you' (16:7). Throughout the gospel 'to see' Jesus means to have faith in him. What Mark is saying is that if the community is to 'see' Jesus, now the Risen One, it must become involved in the mission to the world that 'Galilee' signifies. Galilee was the place of mission, the arena where Jesus' exorcisms and healing had broken the bonds of evil. There, too, the disciples had been called and commissioned to take up Jesus' proclamation of the coming rule of God. 'Galilee' is the place of the universal mission, but no disciples are ready to proclaim the gospel there until they have walked the way to Jerusalem (10:32-4) and encountered the reality of the cross.

Come to Serve

The death of Jesus was wholly consonant with his understanding of authority. He was the one who had come to serve. And if he *spoke* of renouncing self, being least, and losing one's life, his *doing* of all these things lent unanswerable authority to his words. Mark sees clearly (as Paul, before him, had grasped) that the death of Jesus set the seal of authenticity on every single word and deed of his. Mark makes this point, superbly, by presenting the death of Jesus as a disaster, without any relieving feature at all. 'Jesus' death is the supreme moment of illumination in the story. The narrator leads the reader to see in it the ultimate paradox of God's rule, that the anointed one is king not in spite of but precisely because of his loss of life for others. Only when Jesus had "died like this" does the narrative allow a human character in the story to acknowledge Jesus as son of God (15:39); for it is by dying for the good news that Jesus fulfils his role as son of God.'[11]

Mark's story of Jesus and of his way tells us much of Mark himself. We can be sure that he was a man wholly devoted to Jesus of Nazareth. And the Jesus of his faith was a whole human being. His Jesus was never a man of violence but he was one who had challenged the religious establishment of his day. He lashed out at a Temple which set a premium on ritual and jealously reserved a Hebrew God for Hebrews only. He chided a Synagogue which had set law above love. His statement: 'The sabbath was made for man, not man for the sabbath' (2:27)—in translation, 'Religion is for men and women, not men and women for religion'—is subversive of religious systems. It is a word that the Christian Churches have often conveniently forgotten. We owe a debt to Mark for bringing it before us.

It is a saying of the Lord that had appealed to this no-nonsense man. Just like the challenge: 'If any man would come after me, let him deny himself and take up his cross and follow me' (8:34). A reading of his gospel will convince one that Mark's pilgrimage was not a joyless journey to martyrdom. His Jesus did not embrace suffering, did not want to die—the poignant Gethsemane scene makes that much clear (14:32-6). Mark's own attitude would not have been different. But he accepted that the disciple is not greater than his master. Suffering and death are inevitable features of human life. Mark was one who never imagined that the Christian pilgrimage is a luxury cruise. His gospel points us to Galilee: 'there you will see him' (16:7)—a Galilee reached by way of the Cross.

LUKE—*Scriba Mansuetudinis Christi*

Luke was a second-generation Christian who wrote about AD 80-85. Though a Gentile convert (for so it seems) he was concerned with Israel and fully acknowledged the place of Israel in salvation history. He did not look to an imminent parousia; his two-volume work (Gospel and Acts) was written for Christians who lived in the post-apostolic age. 'Today', 'now', is the time of salvation; *now* life is poured out in the Holy Spirit. But now, too, is the time of *ecclesia pressa*, a Church under stress. Luke has shown what may be made of Jesus' deeds and words in a time after the era of Jesus. For us of the late twentieth century, conscious of a gap of two millennia between the first proclamation of the Christian message and our own striving to assimilate that message, Luke's form of the kerygma may be more congenial than others.

To appreciate Luke's purpose and achievement, his Acts of the Apostles, no less than his Gospel, must be taken into account. Then one can see that his object is to present the definitive stage of God's saving plan from the birth of the Baptist to the proclaiming of the gospel in the capital of the Gentile world—Rome. Acts is not, in the first place, a history of the Church; its first concern is the spread of the word of God. Luke's theme is the progress of the Good News from Jerusalem to Rome. His is a message of salvation to the Gentiles. Simeon had seen in Jesus 'a light for revelation to the Gentiles' (Lk 2:32) and Paul's last words to the Roman Jews are: 'Let it be known to you that the salvation of God has been sent to the Gentiles: they will listen' (Acts 28:28).

This concern does not eclipse the role of Israel. The beginning of the gospel attests that the Church does not replace Israel. Himself come from Judaism, Jesus had striven, with the help of the Holy Spirit, to *renew* Israel. The salvation which he proclaimed and achieved meant that one be brought to God. He found that the marginalised—Galileans, women, 'sinners'—were more open to his challenge than the Judaeans and their leaders. But this offer was to all, for Israel needed saving as much as the Gentiles.

In the gospel, after his account of the infancies of John and of Jesus, Luke turns to the preaching of the rule of God first by

131

the precursor and then by the Messiah. At the close of his work he has Paul proclaiming the kingdom at the centre of the Roman world (Acts 28:30-31). The gospel tells of the mission of Jesus and of the saving event of his death and resurrection; it ends with his glorification at the ascension. Jesus had come as Messiah of his people and had found himself rejected by them. But his mission had not failed. He had brought salvation (Lk 24:47).

Minister of the Word

What the Lucan kerygma proclaims is Jesus Christ himself. Jesus had declared that he and his preaching were the fulfilment of what in the Scriptures was associated with God's salvation. He stressed the radical character of the reaction to his kingdom-preaching (16:16); he proclaimed 'salvation' (9:2). Christians perceived that salvation was in him; the subject of their kingdom-preaching was Jesus himself: the crucified, risen and exalted Messiah and the Lord who is present to his followers through his Spirit. Luke has told the story of the Christ-event: Christ proclaimed in his fullness.

Luke, a minister of the word (1:2), an evangelist, has remained faithful to the general plan of his pioneering predecessor, Mark. He has, however, made important changes in this order and so has given to his gospel quite another bias. He has prefaced the Marcan material with the long infancy narrative (chs 1-2) which, as an overture to the gospel, sounds many of the motifs to be orchestrated in Gospel and Acts. In short, one must acknowledge that, despite general agreement with Mark and Matthew, the third gospel is assertively distinctive. This is only to be expected. An evangelist, addressing a *Christian* community, is not telling the Jesus-story for the first time. The original readers knew the lines of the story quite as well as the evangelist. What gave them pause was the question: why is the story presented in just *this* way? The challenge of the evangelist lay, precisely, in the distinctive slant.

Salvation History

Luke is a theologian of salvation history—the entrance of salvation into history. He alludes to a basic divine 'plan' for the salvation of humankind, one which was being realised in the

132

activity of Jesus (7:30). The concept of such a plan is what underlies the necessity (e.g. 'was it not necessary that the Christ should suffer these things and enter into his glory', 24:26) which is often associated with what Jesus does or says and with what happens as the fulfilment of Scripture. That the plan of God concerns the 'salvation' of humankind receives special emphasis in the Lucan writings. Luke alone among the synoptists gives Jesus the title 'Saviour' (2:11).

Salvation had come with Jesus. After the ascension men and women would be saved through him and because of what he had accomplished. The events of the life of Jesus were decisive for the world, constituting the beginning of the last days. For Luke, Jesus was fulfilment of all the promises and that in spite of the outward circumstances of his life which blinded the eyes of his contemporaries to the reality in their presence. This implied that all that went before Jesus was preparatory. Yet, preparation, fulfilment in Christ, and eventual universal salvation through him in this age together form one divine plan for the salvation of the world, a plan progressively realised in history.

Luke has told the Jesus-story not only with christological but with soteriological intent: what Jesus did, said and suffered had and has a significance for and a bearing on human history. Acts 4:12 makes this clear: 'There is salvation in no one else, for there is no other name under heaven given among humankind by which we must be saved'. It has been argued that Luke downplayed 'the cross'. In fact, reference to the death of Jesus in the Lucan writings is impressive. Luke does not seek to suppress the tragedy and mystery of the cross nor to underplay its saving role. He does not question the need for the disciple of Jesus to deny oneself, to take up the cross and follow the Master (9:23; 14:27).

Then there is the manner in which Luke regards the effects of the Christ-event. 'Salvation' is, evidently, an important effect. What he means by it is best summed up in a saying of Jesus: 'The son of man came to seek and to save the lost' (19:10). While the verbal form 'to forgive sins' is frequent in the Synoptics, the abstract form 'forgiveness of sins' is a Lucan usage. Luke sums up Jesus' work as the release of men and women from their debts (sins) in the sight of God. By all that he was and all that he did he has cancelled the debt incurred by their sinful conduct. In the sayings of Jesus 'peace' stands for the bounty that he brings to humankind. And if he seems to deny that his coming brings peace (12:51), it is because he knows that men and women will have to make a decision about him, either for or against him. Those who accept him into their lives will know that peace which he alone can bring.

Dante named Luke *scriba mansuetudinis Christi*—the writer who had caught and portrayed the sensitivity of Jesus. His Jesus had found in Isaiah 61:1-2 the programme of his mission. In his Nazareth synagogue Jesus opened the scroll of Isaiah and read out:

> The Spirit of the Lord is upon me.
> because he has anointed me to preach good news to the
>   poor.
> He has sent me to proclaim release to the captives
> and recovering of sight to the blind.
> to set at liberty those who are oppressed,
> to proclaim the acceptable year of the Lord.

Then he declared: 'Today this scripture has been fulfilled in your hearing' (Lk 18-19, 21). The Lucan Jesus displays gracious concern for the 'little ones'. Instances leap to mind: the raising of a poor widow's son (7:11-17), welcome of the 'lost son' (15:11-24), healing of a crippled woman (13:10-17). Most eloquent, perhaps, is the extravagant and brave gesture of the woman who had experienced the understanding and forgiving love of Jesus (7:36-50). Throughout the gospel there is an unmistakeable apprehension before the threat of affluence and a corresponding sensitivity to the plight of the poor. While there is no need to imagine that this attitude, so evident in the Lucan gospel, does not, in the long run, go back to the teaching of Jesus, it is clear that Luke had made it his own and sees it as an imperative need of the Christian community for which he writes. There is great gentleness, but there is nothing soft or easy-going about this Jesus of Luke. Indeed, there is something almost shocking about the call for total renunciation, his invitation to give up *all* one has. It is certainly shocking in light of his Church's historical pact with capitalism. The demand is prepared for by sharp warnings on the danger of riches. Luke is far more emphatic than the other evangalists on this score: 6:24-6; 12:13-21; 14:33; 14:9; 11:10-31; 18:22. The parable of the Rich Fool carries the moral: 'So is he who lays up treasure for himself, and is not rich towards God.' A choice *must* be made for no one can *serve* God and Mammon (16:13). On the positive side there is the fact that Jesus lived among the poor. At his birth it was shepherds who came to him (2:8), not the Magi of Matthew. His mother gave the offering of the poor (2:24). In short, it is above all in the humble birth of the son of God and in the penury of his life that *voluntary* poverty finds meaning: 'Foxes have holes, and the birds of the air have nests, but the Son of man has nowhere to lay his head' (9:58).

The Lucan attitude to material possessions is not uncomplicated. One may discern a twofold stance: a moderate approach which advocates a prudent use of material possessions in favour of the less fortunate as a response to the message of Jesus and a radical approach which recommends the renunciation of all wealth and possessions. One feels that Luke's own attitude is quite simple: the only sensible thing to do with money is to give it away in alms. No doubt he had in mind the Graeco-Romans among his community who (unlike their Jewish brothers and sisters) had no tradition of almsgiving. But Luke is honest enough to acknowledge that his is not the only view and he leaves place, in his gospel, for a moderate attitude. Luke's somewhat ambivalent stance is not unique in the New Testament. A lesson we might well re-learn from the earliest Christian theologians is a lesson of theological broadmindedness. New Testament writers are not shy of propagating their views, but they had—to the consternation of some present-day Christians—a generous toleration of contrary views. They had the wisdom to realise that there are many ways of being Christian. (There were exceptions!) Some of us, it seems, have disastrously confused unity with uniformity. It is obvious that, in Acts, Paul is Luke's hero. Luke would have been reasonably familiar with Paul's teaching and would have been aware that Paul had not at all advocated the radical repudiation of possessions that was his (Luke's) ideal. In the gospel Luke has proposed his own position. And his radical demand remains a valid Christian option. It was embraced by Francis of Assisi. And it still stands as challenge to one who shares Luke's conviction. The New Testament as a whole demonstrates that Luke's valid insight is not the only Christian view. To be a Christian, one does not *have* to renounce all one has. But one must, at least, be clear that no juggling of New Testament texts can be made to justify the amorality of our western consumer society.

The Way

So much for the 'third gospel'. What of Acts of the Apostles? Regularly, Acts has been presented as political apologetic: to defend or justify the Christian movement in face of Roman political authorities. Or, again, it has been presented as ecclesial apologetic: to explain the Empire in favourable terms to Luke's fellow Christians and so to encourage them to adopt a positive stance towards Rome. Both views are wide of Luke's intent. Luke's purpose should be labelled: allegiance-witness, that is to say, commitment to Jesus and the courageous living-out of that commitment. Jesus had faced up with courage and dignity to Jewish and Roman authorities. Paul (in Acts) did nothing less. Of particular interest is Paul's attitude to Roman authorities and his estimation of his Roman citizenship: subordinate to his Jewishness and to his vocation as a witness to and servant of Jesus Christ. In short, he mirrored Jesus' stance in face of the Roman order.[12]

Luke's spirituality is firmly inspired by his commitment to Jesus—that much is obvious. What matters is his commitment to the Jesus he *recognised*. And here is where Dante's observation is perceptively true. The Jesus of Luke is—though the title occurs only once (2:11)—Saviour. God's 'preferential option for the poor' might seem to be a new-fangled invention of Liberation theology. In fact, it is a belated re-discovery of an option that was there from the first. No put-down of Liberation theology; rather, a heartfelt 'thank you' to Liberation theologians for opening our eyes to what we should never have failed to see. The Lucan Jesus does indeed reflect the God who, one hopes, has emerged clearly in our Old Testament sketches. He is, disconcertingly, God of sinners. Apart from the so-called judgment-scene of Matthew 25:31-46, there is no passage more subversive of Christian 'orthodoxy' than Luke 15:11-32. A 'sinner' is welcomed back into the home of his Father, welcomed without strings, welcomed at the word: 'I will arise and go'. The Father-God had yearned for an opening—he needed no more. Some time or other the Church, so readily arbiter of 'reconciliation', must learn that the Father of Jesus is prodigal of forgiveness. Let us be honest about it: bishops and theologians have multiplied 'sins'; at least they did so in the past, even the recent past. The God of Jesus knows that there is enough human misery and sin as it is. The Lucan Jesus, who truly knows the Father, is wholly in the business of lifting the burden of sin—not of adding to it. That is why Jesus is Saviour.

What of the journey of Luke? He may have been of Gentile background, but he certainly knew, or came to know, his Bible. He was one who had found, in Jesus, the inspiration and goal of his life. He viewed this Jesus in light of his own temperament. It is evident from his writings that Luke was sensitive and perceptive. It is, obviously, the 'softer' side of the character of Jesus that appealed to him. A distinctive feature of Luke-Acts is the predominance of women in the narrative: more women are listed in Luke than in the other three gospels together. This tells us something not only about Jesus but also about Luke. He, like Jesus and Paul, was not afraid of women. He could relate to women easily, without embarrassment. Luke's sensitivity to the 'poor' is not unrelated: in the world of his day women were among the poor, the marginalised. In the same spirit he was concerned for 'outcast' Samaritans (10:30-37; 17:11-19). After all, Jesus had come 'to preach good news to the poor' (4:18).

HEBREWS—*Journey towards the City to Come*

The splendid letter to the Hebrews was written by an unknown, immensely gifted, hellenistic Christian to encourage Jewish Christians who, in face of difficulties and persecution, were tempted to drift from Christianity. The author exhorts them to cling to the Word of God as revealed in Christ and to persevere in faith. The force of the argument rests on the person and work of Jesus: Son of God, eternal high priest, offering a perfect sacrifice. Hebrews is most likely a document of the second Christian generation and may be reasonably dated in the eighties.

The central theme of Hebrews, the priesthood of Christ is formulated in terms of Jewish theological categories: Christ is superior to angels, to Moses, to the levitical preisthood, and Christ's sacrifice is superior even to the high-priestly liturgy of the Day of Atonement. Such Old Testament concepts were well appreciated by first-century Jewish converts—though perhaps not, even then, by all; inevitably, they lose something of their relevance after nineteen centuries. Nonetheless we happen, throughout the letter, on religious truths of perennial validity. The author meant his treatise to be 'a word of exhortation' (13:22). The whole is a fine statement of the saving work of Christ and is for our day a moving word of exhortation in a time when we may be tempted to 'fall away from the living God' (2:12).

Towards a Resting-Place

A special worth of Hebrews is its contribution to christology. For the author, Jesus is Son of God; but he is the Son who 'had to be made like his brethren in every respect' (2:17), a Son who 'in every respect has been tempted as we are, yet without sinning' (4:15). He is the human being who stands in a relationship of obedient faithfulness towards God (3:16) and who stands in solidarity with human suffering. Thereby he is a mediator: true priest who can bring humankind to God. If he bears 'the very stamp of God's nature' (1:3) it is because we see in him what makes God God; he shows us that God is God humankind. But he is a God to whom we must give heed: we must listen to his word *today*. In 3:7-4:11 the infidelity of Israel in the desert—they did not listen to the word—serves as an eloquent warning to Christians. The whole is a commentary on Psalm 95:7-11: under Moses an unfaithful generation was punished by exclusion from the temporal rest of Canaan; much more must Christians fear the apostasy which would exclude them from eternal rest. Apostasy is seen as a threat hanging over the community of 'Hebrews': 'Take care, brethren, lest there be in any of you an evil, unbelieving heart, leading you to fall away [literally, "apostatise"] from the living God' (3:12).

From the tenor of the letter one gathers, we have noted, that a community of Jewish Christians (or some among them) were being tempted to return to their former religious allegiance. The author counters the temptation by painting it as a retrograde step from substance to shadow. Moreover, apostasy evokes the threat of eschatological judgment. Specifically, in our passage, the author plays on the term 'rest'—meaning rest in the presence of God. He insists that this rest can be achieved only through sharing in Christ (v. 14). The people of Moses had journeyed towards 'rest'. But not even under Joshua did they achieve rest. Hence, the promise of entrance into rest still stands open. Cleverly, the author has argued from a psalm-text much later than the time of Joshua: 'Again he sets a certain day, "Today", saying through David so long afterwards, in the words already quoted, "Today, when you hear his voice, do not harden your hearts." For if Joshua had given them rest, God would not speak of another day' (4:7-8). Today is *now:* the challenge is addressed to this generation: 'Let *us* therefore strive to enter that rest, that no one fall by the same sort of disobedience' (4:11).

Pilgrimage

The use by our author of the imagery of the wilderness wanderings and of the idea of 'rest', however superficial some of his arguments from the biblical texts may seem, reflects some of his deepest convictions and expresses some of his fundamental attitudes towards the Christian life. For him life is a struggle, fittingly concluded by a sabbath rest. He does not think of the people of God as inhabiting city dwellings built upon firm foundations, but rather as living like nomads in tents, looking forward to the city that is to come. In this transient world there is no ultimate security, no final achievement, no objective fulfilment. The vision of the end gives encouragement to brave the inevitable hardships of the Christian pilgrimage. Travellers are heartened by the knowledge that their leader who has gone before them and who has made their journey possible has himself shared the human weaknesses with

139

which pilgrims are beset... Our author gives moral admonitions which might be termed 'a highway code' to keep them moving in a body towards their goal.[13]

There is, then, a pilgrimage. And there is the reassurance that one has reached the goal: 'Since then we have a great high priest who has passed through the heavens, Jesus, the Son of God. Let us hold fast our confession' (4:14). If he, 'like us in every respect' (2:17), rejoices in the presence of God—his 'rest'—then we, with him (and only with him) can find our place, too, before 'the throne of grace' (4:16). Christian life is pilgrimage: 'For we have here no lasting city, but we seek the city which is to come' (13:14). (Paul had said as much: 'Our homeland is in heaven', Phil 3:20). We are sojourners. But the Christian pilgrimage is not an aimless wandering; we journey, in confidence, to a secure destination. The author tells his readers: You no longer belong to the old covenant but to the new. Look no more to Sinai but to the heavenly Jerusalem and its atmosphere of assurance and hope. More than hope, for you already possess the good things of the new dispensation; you already have your visa for entry into the heavenly Jerusalem (ch. 12). And, throughout that journey you are in the care of 'our Lord Jesus Christ, the great Shepherd' (13:20).

Forerunners and Leader
The consistently negative evaluation of the whole levitical system might suggest that, for the author of Hebrews, the Old Testament holds nothing of value for Christians. Not so: there is, among other things, the inspiring example of the faith of the great men and women of Israel. The patriarchs (Abraham, Isaac, Jacob) had 'acknowledged that they were strangers and exiles on the earth. People who speak thus make it clear that they are seeking a homeland... they desire a better country, that is, a heavenly one' (11:13-16). The realisation that the saints of the Old Testament, their noble ancestors in the faith, are witnesses of the great race which Christians must run will give the Jewish Christians heart and encourage them to persevere (12:1-2). Nor are these merely interested spectators. As in a relay race, the first runners have passed on the baton of faith—they are deeply involved in the outcome of this race of

Christians. But the example that is best calculated to sustain the patience and courage of Christians is that of their Lord who was humiliated and crucified only to rise again and enter into his glory. Jesus is the 'pioneer'—that is, chief and leader—offering the example of a faith strong enough to enable him to endure the trials of his whole life. 'Looking to Jesus' is the kernel of the letter.

JOHN—a House Divided

It does not take long to recognise that the Johannine Jesus is, in many respects, very different from the Jesus of the synoptists, nor that the Fourth Gospel is notably different from their gospels. It is not only a question of style but of content and, especially, of christology. True, John and the synoptists tell the same story, but they tell it differently. While already in Matthew and Luke there is a tendency to stress what one might call the other-worldliness of Jesus, in John he seems something of a sojourner from another world. In the synoptics Jesus' message concerns 'the Kingdom of God', the benevolent rule of God. In John what Jesus preaches, what he reveals, is himself. Jesus is still concerned to make the real God known, but now who God is can be known and seen in Jesus himself. True, it is in and through Jesus we come to know God, but the Johannine emphasis is distinctive: 'No one has ever seen God, the only Son who is in the bosom of the Father, he has made him known' (Jn 1:18). There is a series of 'I am' sayings (e.g. 'I am the bread of life', 'I am the light of the world', 'I am the resurrection and the life'—6:35; 8:12; 11:25). This reaches its height in the four absolute I AM sayings (8:24, 28, 58; 13:19). Each time there is a conscious echo of the divine name of Exodus 3:14. We should not, however, lose sight of the fact that, throughout the Fourth Gospel, Jesus' subordination to the Father is just as clearly expressed (e.g. 6:19; 5:26). And 14:28 states bluntly: 'The Father is greater than I'. This qualifying aspect of Johannine christology has rarely been given its proper weight.

The Fourth Gospel had a complex genesis and grew in

141

stages. Yet, it shows signs of having been moulded by a dominant figure who shaped the traditional material to a particular theological cast and expression. We can be sure that, for the Johannine community, another than he, the 'Beloved Disciple' (cf. 13:23; 19:26-27; 20:2-9; 21:7, 20-23), a disciple during Jesus' ministry, and source of the tradition, was the greatly-venerated link with Jesus; he stands, in contrast to Peter, as the father-figure of the Johannine group. The gospel may have taken its final shape in Ephesus (where the Letters, too, would have been written). Its likely date: AD 90-100.

Turmoil

The Fourth Gospel shows signs of turmoil within the community, largely over christology. The first Johannine Christians were, all of them, Jews who lived within the synagogue structure. They acknowledged Jesus as the fulfilment of Israel's hope and strenuously proclaimed their conviction. They maintained that Jesus was immeasurably superior to all of the religious figures of Israel—even Abraham and Moses. In debate with their fellow Jews they further pressed their claims for Jesus. He is *the* Word of God (1:1) who alone had seen God 91:18; 6:46). Indeed, Jesus is 'equal to God' (5:18; 10:33) and can assume the name of God: I AM. For 'orthodox' Jews such claims were intolerable: one could not make such claims for Jesus and remain within the synagogue. In the Johannine community, as in the early Christian communities in general, the tragic moment was when Christianity broke free of its roots—perhaps, more accurately, when Judaism could no longer accommodate the disciples of Jesus of Nazareth.

Schism

The Johannine Christians found themselves expelled from the synagogue. In chapter 9 of John the parents of the man born blind will not be drawn into the quarrel 'because they feared the Jews, for the Jews had already agreed that if any one should confess him to be Christ, he was to be put out of the synagogue' (9:22, cf. 9:34). The same evidence emerges from 12:42; 16:2. A more bitter blow was when some within the community found the claim that Jesus was a descended heavenly being too much to take—they left (6:61-6). 'Many of his disciples said . . . this is a hard saying; who can listen to it? . . . After this many of his disciples went back and no longer went about with him.' Those who remained hardened their christological stance. For one thing, their emphasis on Jesus as one 'descended' from the heavenly world came to mean that he was 'not of this world' (cf. 17:16). Stress on the otherworldliness of Jesus meant that the significance of his life and death was obscured—a fact that surfaces in the Johannine Letters. These Letters tell of a further schism—again over the christological issue. And this is a very good reason why the gospel should be taken in close association with the Letters. It would seem, in fact, that the author of 1 John was largely responsible for having the Fourth Gospel eventually accepted by the Church at large.

Come in the Flesh

In 1 John 2:18 the author, using apocalyptic language, asserts that the appearance of 'antichrists' signals the 'last hour'—the 'antichrists' being those Johannine Christians who had broken with the author's party. In 2 John 7 we have the equivalent of the 'antichrist' text of 1 John 2:19—the 'deceivers and antichrists' will not acknowledge 'the coming of Jesus Christ in the flesh'. In contrast, true believers 'confess that Jesus Christ has come in the flesh' (1 Jn 4:2-3). Manifestly, the issue is 'come in the flesh'. Refusal to acknowledge 'coming in the flesh' does not mean a denial of the incarnation—the 'secessionists' (a convenient term for the breakaway group) are not docetists. The trouble with the secessionists is that they have pushed high christology a stage too far. For them the entry of the heavenly figure into our world—the Word-made-flesh—was, by itself, the saving event; the life and death of Jesus had no saving significance. They took their stand on an interpretation of the Johannine tradition which the author of the Letters regarded as misinterpretation. He insists on the saving importance of the life and death of Jesus (1:7, 2:2, 4:9-10; 5:6).

The Johannine letters illustrate all too sadly that charity is the first victim of fraternal polemic. These former brethren are now not only antichrists but haters of the brethren (1:9-11),

143

murderers like Cain (3:12), children of the devil (3:8-10) who belong to the faithless world (4:5). The true believers will have nothing to do with them (2 John 10). The author of the Letters, who stresses love so, proves singularly unloving towards those whom he regarded as deserters—or who could not share his theology.[14]

A Troubled Road

The Johannine Christians walked a troubled pilgrimage. They were Jews who had come to terms with their growing christological appreciation of Jesus. Their faith in him as Risen One was a challenge to their monotheistic faith. He was not Yahweh. Yet, as the 'one sent', as plenipotentiary of the Father, he could speak in the name of that Father, could utter the I AM. He was WORD: he spoke the presence of God in the world of humankind. Their claims for Jesus had to be wholly unacceptable to their Jewish brothers and sisters who did not share their faith. Their christological pilgrimage took them on a journey from the synagogue into a separate community—into a new religion. Further christological tension brought them to another parting of ways. For some of them the claims for Jesus had gone too far: 'After this many of his disciples drew back and no longer went about with him' (Jn 6:66). The pilgrimage did not end there. Exponents of an ultra-high christology broke with their 'conservative' brothers and sisters and went their way—ultimately into Gnosticism. The others (seemingly a minority) eventually, if reluctantly, merged with the early Church. Without that merger it is likely that the Fourth Gospel, beloved of Gnostics, would have been lost to Christianity.

The troubled Johannine story supports the comforting evidence that there never has been a perfect Christian community. Our more searching study, in recent times, of the New Testament has brought to light hitherto undiscerned tension and strife. I would regard this awareness not as cause for discouragement but as hope and promise. A model of *perfect* Christians offers no hope at all to frail and sinful humans. A reality of squabbling Christians—right from the start—does offer promise. Our Christian religion is geared to our needs, the needs of men and women, not yet fully human, yet all too human!

144

JESUS OF NAZARETH—*a Man on the Move*

'Let us run with perseverance the race that is set before us, looking to Jesus the pioneer and perfecter of our faith' (Heb 12:1-2). For the author of Hebrews faith in Jesus, the High Priest 'seated at the right hand of the throne of God' (12:2), is what gives meaning to the Christian Way. At the same time, perhaps no other New Testament writer has stressed more than he the humanity of this heavenly high priest. For, he has in sight a specific historical person: Jesus of Nazareth. Christianity is not founded on myth. Yet, what came to be, after New Testament times, was ahistorical christology displaying little of the vulnerable Jesus who died on a cross. Even when the earthly Jesus was kept in view there has been a tendency to detach the death of Jesus from his life and to detach the resurrection of Jesus from his career and death. To do so is to ignore the challenge of the prophet Jesus, and, ultimately, to fail to grasp the saving significance of his death and the true meaning of his resurrection. The life of Jesus of Nazareth is the key to what Christianity is all about. Logically, this section might have been expected after the piece on the Baptist. It is surely more fitting to hold the supreme Hero to the last.

For Jesus, too, life was pilgrimage—at more than one level. What Luke said of the twelve-year-old is perceptively true: 'And Jesus increased in wisdom and in stature and in favour with God and man' (2:52). His journey was not only from Nazareth to the Jordan, from Galilee to Jerusalem. It was, above all, a journey of faith. Jesus, who knew the Father as no other did, still had to learn what it was the Father asked of him at the end of all. While fully aware that, in everything he did and said, he revealed the true God, he was to find that his last word was to be the revelation of what Paul would term the 'foolishness' of God. The man himself was the revelation; his life and his death the medium of his message.

The Rule of God

Jesus came into Galilee preaching the kingdom of God and saying, 'The time is fulfilled and the Kingdom of God is at hand' (Mk 1:14-15).

145

Jesus proclaimed the *basileia,* the rule of God. In simple terms, he proclaimed the love of God as this unconditional and liberating love finds living expression in the lives of men and women. In no other way can God's rule become reality. It found shape in the life of Jesus. He 'went about, doing good'; he championed the outcast, he welcomed and pardoned sinners. Jesus, in his life-style, gave concrete expression to the good life—a life worthy of humankind. He demonstrated that the kingdom is meant to be a reality within our world.

> The kingdom of God is a new relationship of human beings to God, with as its tangible and visible side a new type of liberating relationship between men and women, within a peaceful, reconciled society.... It is a new world of suffering removed, a world of completely whole or healed men and women in a society where master-servant relationships no longer prevail, quite different from life under Roman occupation. Precisely at this point Jesus turns especially to the poor.... These in particular are the ones whom Jesus sought out, and he ate with them. In all this Jesus was aware that he was acting as God would do. He translates God's action for men and women.... Jesus acts as God acts. So he embodies a claim that in his actions and words God himself is present. To act as God does is praxis of the kingdom of God and also shows what the kingdom of God is: salvation for men and women.[15]

In preaching the rule of God Jesus was defining God. He was proclaiming a God bent on the salvation of humankind. This is why he announced good news to the poor—the needy of every sort, the outcast. That is why he was friend of sinners, why he had tablefellowship with them.

Luke has Jesus open his ministry in the Nazareth synagogue. Historical or not, it is an appropriate setting and the Isaian text which he chose surely mapped the programme he was to follow:

> The Spirit of the Lord is upon me, because he has anointed me to preach good news to the poor. He has sent me to proclaim release to the captives and recovering of sight to the blind, to set at liberty those who are

oppressed, to prolcaim the acceptable year of the Lord (Lk 4:18-19; cf. Is 61:1-2).

His 'preferential option for the poor' was not an exclusive option because, for him, 'poor' embraced the whole of humanity. Those most in need were those who did not know their need. Jesus did not shun his opponents: he dialogued with them.

Nonetheless, his warm concern for the poor—the 'little ones'—brought him into conflict with those whose understanding of God was so different from his. Because he would not brand anyone an outcast, because he put ethics in place of preoccupation about ritual, because he set people above observance, he was classed as a breaker of the Law, as one who did not do the will of God. He remained faithful to the God he knew and he responded to the will of his loving Father—though that faithfulness was to take him to the cross.

Jesus had begun his mission with optimism. He did not start off with a grim vision of violent death at the end of the road. But, as his career progressed, he had to come to terms with the reaction and opposition that forced him to reckon with, first, the possibility and, then, the probability, of violent death. It is likely that the temptation stories, put at the start of the ministry by Matthew and Luke, really concern decisions made at a later stage. There is no doubt that Gethsemane and the anguished cry from the cross witness to the agony of decision and the depressing prospect of failure.

Journey to Death

In his gosepl plan, Mark has a journey of Jesus from Galilee to Jerusalem (10:32-11:25) a journey set at a pretty brisk pace. In Luke the journey is a leisurely stroll, so leisurely that, though Jesus had resolutely 'set his face to go to Jerusalem'—and had indeed set out—by 9:51, not until 19:28-40 (ten chapters down the road) did he enter the city. What has happened is that Luke has cleverly exploited that Marcan journey and has used it as a framework for a whole block of Jesus' teaching. What really matters is that this journey from Galilee to Jerusalem was the most important pilgrimage in human history. After all, there can be no more significant journey than that from life to death and the march of Jesus of Nazareth from his friendly Galilee to the Jerusalem of his enemies (that is how Mark viewed it) was a march to death. That is not what Jesus had wanted it to be. His Gethsemane prayer ('remove this cup from me', Mk 14:36) makes that much clear.

The pilgrimage of Jesus—*the* representative of our God—from a ministry of uninhibited love of humankind to the helpless victim of humankind on a human-provided cross, is the great and the ultimate human pilgrimage. No banners there, no colourful procession—despite an ephemeral welcome (Mk 11:1-10; par.). Just disillusionment, shared by followers: 'Jesus was walking ahead of them; and they were amazed, and those who followed were afraid' (Mk 10:32). They had caught the smell of disaster; the scent was clear enough. Popular enthusiasm had waned: Jesus was no messianic warrior but a pacifist for the cause of God. Yet, he had explicitly challenged the religious establishment by his criticism of Temple worship and of Pharisaic observance of Torah. He was a heretic. He had implicitly challenged Rome. He was a rebel. It did not matter that his challenge was totally peaceful and wholly marked by love. He was walking the most precarious walk of all: the walk of one who holds for love in face of those who acknowledge only power—whether naked or subtly disguised. That awesome, and awful, journey to the Cross is comfort to all who have seen in Jesus of Nazareth the image of the invisible God; it is the consolation of all who have found in him the ultimate assurance that God is on *our* side.

Jesus had 'set his face to go to Jerusalem' (Lk 9:51). Mark's Gethsemane-scene (14:32-42) shows that he did not fully understand God's way, shows that he did not want to die. His Gethsemane decision was to trust God despite the darkness of his situation. He entrusted to God his own experience of failure: his endeavour to renew Israel was being brutally thwarted. His cry of God-forsakenness on the cross—'My God, my God, why have you forsaken me?'—speaks the bitterness of his sense of failure. Jesus had not set out from Galilee to embrace the cross. Throughout his ministry he had preached the rule of God—God as salvation for humankind. His last, involuntary, sermon was the most eloquent of all. The close of

148

his earthly pilgrimage was to be his unequivocal proclamation of true divinity and true humanity. For, the cross is God's revelation of himself. It is there he defines himself over against all human caricatures of him. God, in the cross, is a radical challenge to our *hubris,* our pride. There he is seen to be the *Deus humanissimus*—the God wholly bent on the salvation of humankind. No wonder that Paul can ask, in awe: 'Since God did not withold from us the most precious of all gifts, even the life of his own Son to give life to us all, can we not be certain that he would not possibly refuse us whatever else we may need' (Rom 8:32).

The cross does not only say much about God; it says a great deal about humankind. There God's Son dramatically demonstrates the radical powerlessness of the human being. He shows us that we are truly human when we accept our humanness, when we face up to the fact that we are not masters of our fate. As Jesus was stripped of his clothes, so too, he displays a humanness stripped of every illusion. On the cross Jesus manifested himself as the one who had yielded himself wholly to his God. The cross offers the only authentic definition of humankind: God's definition. Man is creature—but only so that God may be wholly with him as Creator. Or, to put it no less truly but more intimately: he is child, that God may be with him as Father/Mother.[16]

Jesus lived—and died. His life is the explanation of his death. He had lived for humankind; he died for us. Jesus laid down his life in loving response to the Father's love. The Father did not demand the death of Jesus; the Father did not need the death of Jesus. The Father gave his Son for humankind, but gave him *eis telos*—in steadfast love to the last. He would show human beings that his love for them was in deadly earnest. The Father did not bring about the death of his Son; Jesus died at the hands of his religious and political enemies. But the Father did not shrink from having him 'delivered up' to his enemies. Only so does the death of Jesus fall within 'the definite plan and foreknowledge of God' (Acts 2:23). And, in filial acceptance of God's saving purpose, and only so, did Jesus accept death. He was obedient unto death—with an obedience that was a loving 'Yes' to a purpose of sheerest love. 'God so loved the world...'. There is no gainsaying that word. It is the only explanation of the death of Jesus that is consonant with the character of our God.

The career of Jesus did not end on the cross. The resurrection is God's endorsement of the definitions of both God and humankind which became real on the cross. For, just as the death of Jesus cannot be detached from his life, so too his resurrection cannot be detached from his career and death. Because he was raised from the dead, Jesus holds decisive significance for us. Because of the fact of his resurrection we know that meaningless death (and, often, meaningless life) now have meaning. Jesus died with the cry on his lips: 'My God, my God, why have you abandoned me?' The sequel was to show that God had never abandoned Jesus. We have the assurance that he will never abandon us. Unlike his immediate disciples, we do not follow the steps of Jesus from Galilee to Jerusalem. We do join his human pilgrimage from birth to death. His word of promise is that we shall follow him beyond death to share his rest (cf. Heb 12:2).

Jesus and the Land

At the start we noted that biblical promise is firmly linked to land: the land of Israel, the land of Galilee and Judaea. Yahweh's covenant with Israel was about land. A prime stipulation of that covenant was concern for the poor. There was no virtue in landlessness, in being poor. If, in later Old Testament times, the *anawim* were the poor who put their trust in God alone, they still, like Simeon, 'looked for the consolation of Israel' (Lk 2:25). Jesus' teaching gives no grounds for the later prevalent notion that poverty, in itself, is virtuous. That notion has powerfully helped to sanction inequity. The poor are not blessed for being poor; they are blessed because to them belongs the kingdom, the new land.

The land is always gift and is always responsibility. It involves promise of God and demands of God. The history of Israel shows varied ways of possessing the land—and of losing it: the way of landlessness in the desert (promise only), the way of the monarchy, the way of Judaism. The land could be lost by grasping at it as though it were Israel's and not God's, through forgetting the stipulations of God and the demands of the land. It mattered not whether the 'land' were soil of Israel, religious establishment, or a kingdom of the future. Always it was gift and always it made demands in the here and now.

Jesus summed up the meaning of the 'land' in his dual command of love of God and love of neighbour. In the astounding judgment scene of Matthew 25:31-46 it has become a single demand. Who will be acknowledged by the Son of Man at his glorious coming? One who had loved the Son of Man in concrete deeds of mercy. The surprise of 'sheep' and 'goats' is utter: 'Lord, when did we see *you*...?' They learn that Jesus has wholly identified himself with the poor and outcast and oppressed, that he is one with *all* in need—they are his brothers and sisters. He makes the Old Testament land-demand of concern for the poor (Lev 25) the primary concern and gives it a christological basis.

A disciple of Jesus is one who does the will of the Father (Mt 12:50). Neglect of the poor is the decisive not-doing of the will of God which excludes from the heritage. The condemned (25:41-45), while not denying their neglect of the suffering, do protest that they never saw Jesus in need. And that is just the point. It is because they had failed to understand Jesus' identification with the needy, the suffering, that the 'goats' had failed to minister to him and to serve him. Those who had perceived the claim of the land and had served the needy hear the invitation: 'Come, O blessed of my Father, inherit the kingdom prepared for you from the foundation of the world' (25:34). They are the meek, the unassuming, the considerate, who inherit the earth (5:5).

Jesus, the crucified one, is the King who utters judgment. But what kind of judgement is this? He is the one who identifies himself with the lowly—with all the daughters and sons of men. He is the loving and living expression of God's concern for humankind. A God bent on humankind, and nothing short of that, becomes the standard of our concern for those in need. That is why just this concern is the criterion of judgment. That is why the words of warning sound so harshly. The 'last judgment' is warning: it primarily relates to one's conduct in the present. We are being taught how we should prepare for the 'coming' of the Lord, prepare for our meeting with him. The author of Hebrews had exhorted the community of his concern, a people on pilgrimage to 'the city which is to come':

151

'Let brotherly love continue. Do not neglect to show hospitality to strangers. . . . Remember those who are in prison, as though in prison with them; and those who are ill-treated, since you also are in the body' (13:1-3). This is the way to the promised rest.

The promise to Abraham was that in him all the nations of the earth would be blessed. The kingdom of David came to be seen, in hope, as a universal kingdom. Jesus would declare that the kingdom of God is among us in that good news is preached to the poor. The promised land was promised to the homeless. The good news is always, first and foremost, good news for the dispossessed, the marginalised. The meek are meant to inherit the earth. It is not enough that Christians should look to the future. Christianity, because it is incarnational, should permeate every aspect of human life. If the Promised Land is not to be found on earth it will not be possessed at all.

Pilgrim
Spirituality

PILGRIM SPIRITUALITY

At the outset I noted the difficulty of coming up with a satisfactory definition of 'spirituality'. This may be because spirituality is not theory but a lived experience and is, in a sense,
unique to a person. Spirituality implies a relationship between
an individual and God—but not lived in lonely isolation. It is a
relationship of faith and love: trust in God and a love reaching
to concern for other men and women. A constant motif
throughout these sketches of biblical men and women has been
that of pilgrimage. If spirituality is lived experience, then
'pilgrimage' will be part of it. One might have brought
together here, by way of conclusion, traits of pilgrimage and
aspects of spirituality. On the whole, it may be less confusing
to handle the themes separately.

Pilgrimage

Noah was a man surprised by God. He could scarcely have
dreamt that he would be called on to embark on a voyage that
was to make his name immortal. His journey was to a
mountain-top—and to a covenant. It was a journey out of
chaos to a fresh beginning and a renewed promise. Abraham
found himself challenged to drop everything and go. There was
no discernible goal as he set out on his seemingly aimless way.
Despite the call and the promise he remained a wanderer all his
days. Jacob had sought to plan his course but had had to flee
into exile when his cunning had recoiled on him. He met God,
fleetingly, on the way. He encountered and came to know his
God when, much later, he was returning to his home-land. As
an old man he had to journey yet: to Joseph and to the land of
Goshen. Moses, too, had to flee for his life. In the land of
refuge he heard the Name of his God. Moses found himself
leading a motley group out of slavery to the mountain of God.
The exodus of Moses has reverberated through the history of
Judaism and of Christianity. The chosen leader did not enter
the Promised Land—suggesting to the author of Hebrews that
another and better rest awaits God's people.

Possession of the land was precarious. The journey may have
ended, but there was no rest. Again we meet one who had to
leave his home—this time driven from it. Jephthah did return:

as master. His victory procession ended in tragedy: the death, by his own hand, of his only daughter. He walked a bitter road, following an erroneous conscience and he must have longed for the repose of Sheol. What is one to make of Samson's amorous strolls and vainglorious forays? In the view of the biblical author the manner of his dying atoned for his folly: 'It is a far, far better thing I do than I have ever done...'. In contrast stands the gentle Ruth who came with her beloved mother-in-law to a land of strangers and to another God. There she found a home—and became ancestress of David.

'I took you from the pasture, from following the sheep, that you should be prince over my people Israel' (2 Sam 7:8). David had to flee the jealous rage of Saul and his early years were spent in wandering. Not aimless wandering; he had shrewdly built a power-base. He ended up king of Judah and, later, king of Judah-and-Israel. There was to be a further flight—before an ambitious son who sought his throne and his life. David had journeyed too from sin to honest repentance and through the maze of family strife. He had served the Lord and had paid the price. Amos the Judaean carried out his mission in the land of Israel—another exile! He fearlessly challenged corruption in high places, and the oppression of the poor. He pitilessly exposed the emptiness behind an elaborate cultic façade. He walked the path of righteousness and summoned others to follow. Hosea walked the road of love. He tasted the sweets of love and the bitterness. He learned that faithfulness in face of unfaithfulness is costly indeed. His own painful journey through love gave him a startling glimpse into the heart of his loving God.

'See, I have set you this day...to pluck up and to break down, to destroy and to overthrow' (Jer 1:10). Jeremiah faced a hopeless task. His road led to failure; he could not bring his people to see the chasm that yawned before them. Despite his best efforts, they blundered into the abyss. Jeremiah, in his manner, walked the way of the cross. His life vividly illustrated the price of faithful service. When disaster struck he switched from woe to hope and spoke of the promise of a new covenant. His contemporary, Ezekiel, had been exiled to Babylon. There he, too, held out hope. There would be a spiritual journey to a new heart and a new spirit. There would be a pilgrimage from

Babylon to a new house of Yahweh.

'Isaiah' spans three or more centuries: a journey indeed! He was theologian of Zion and troubadour of the Exile; he held aloft a banner of hope in a fragile post-exilic Judah. The sixth-century prophet had urged a Return and had painted it, in glowing colours, as a new and magnificent exodus. The reality was a modest happening—but it was *real*. As for the people of 'Isaiah': they had journeyed from complacency to despondency—and on to a pitiful settlement once again in the land. Hope flickered and did not go out. Jonah: a reluctant prophet journeying to an unwelcome goal. He had sought to flee from the Lord—to no avail. He wended his unwilling way to Nineveh, where his worst fears were realised. One may hope that he learned from the experience and shrugged free of his narrow rigidity.

The harrowing journey of Job was from faith to faith. It was an epic journey—though he had not stirred from his seat on the ash-heap. He groped through a dark night, throwing down the gauntlet to that elusive God along the way. His quest for an answer to the perennial problem of innocent suffering is as pressing in our day as ever it was in his. Our perception, not shared by the author of Job, of an afterlife and of retribution beyond death, should not dispose us to find a facile answer to the problem. We should hear Job's challenge and face, as he did, the factor of a seemingly uncaring God. We could do with a share of his faith. Qoheleth raises the unavoidable question of the absurdity of death. It is not alone that the sage and the fool, the wicked man and the saint, meet as equals in Sheol—a dead dog and a dead man are equally dead! Death is the great leveller. Can life, then, hold meaning— Qoheleth clings to his fatih in God but his was a restless spirit. He set out on a journey of the mind: *fides quaerens intellectum.* No more than Job does he find a theoretically satisfying answer at the end of his quest. He found the practically satisfying answer of faith in a God who is on top of his job: 'I know that whatever God does endures forever...I know that it will be well with those who fear God' (Qoh 3:14; 8:12).

The story of Esther tells how a Jewish orphan girl became queen of Persia—a journey from rags to riches. It was much more than that, of course. Her rise was providential: an occasion of salvation for her people. Her uncle's perception was right: 'Who knows whether you have not come to the kingdom for such a time as this?' (Est 4:14). Maiden to queen we have seen. Widow to heroine: that was the path of Judith. Her short walk to the Assyrian siege-lines was to open a way of salvation for her people. It could be that, as for Esther, an unforeseen goal might be a way of liberation for her sisters. Finally, Tobias' journey in search of money held in trust led him to a far more precious treasure: a beloved bride. All because God had heard the prayer of two godly, afflicted ones and had been step by step with Tobias on his way.

John the Baptist steps right out of the Old Testament: an Elijah-figure. His journey took him to the Jordan where he confronted 'all Israel'. He had followed the unrelenting way of Amos. But his path led to Herod's dungeon where his life was taken from him. As precursor he had anticipated the fate of the Coming One. A pregnant Mary journeyed from Nazareth to Bethlehem, where her child was born. She learned in the Temple of the destiny of the child—a sign of contradiction—and shared his exile. She witnessed his death. Her deeper journey was one through the darkness of faith: blessed she who believed. Another Mary was with Jesus on his travels, among his little group of disciples. She, too, was with him at his death. She, Mary Magdalene, was first to meet the Risen One. 'Go to my brethren': a short journey—but a stupendous message.

There is something admirable and comforting about the person who can discern the promise of another and then generously further that other's way. Such a person was Barnabas—an apostle and missionary to whom Paul owed much. Paul himself was the first, and the greatest, *peregrinus pro Christo*. He has written of his missionary travels, leaving no doubt as to their extent and their personal cost to himself (2 Cor 11:21-9). He would readily acknowledge that his greater journey was from Torah to Cross. One who had perceived the Nazarene as a fatal threat to all that Saul held dear was transformed into the most faithful follower of Christ. The evangelist Mark was a kindred spirit. He saw that the Christian journey is not only a carrying of the cross—it finds meaning in the cross. Not until one has come to terms with the death of Jesus, and its meaning, can one truly confess and rightly follow:

'In truth this man was Son of God!' (Mk 15:39).

For Luke the Christian journey is inspired and sustained by the Spirit of the Lord. Even while alone, we are not alone. There is a Guide along every metre of the way. It is a joyous way lit by the graciousness of the one who is our Saviour. That the Christian Way *is* pilgrimage is the emphatic message of the author of Hebrews: we journey towards the City of the future. This is not to say that earthly life is meaningless. If our High Priest does now take his rest in the heavenly Sanctuary, he once walked among us in sweat and tears. 'Therefore let us go forth to him...bearing abuse for him' (Heb 13:13). We must be tried and tested as he was; we must run *our* race. Johannine Christians had begun their journey from within the synagogue. That journey was—surely unforeseen—to take them into another religion. A stage was reached when no longer might the wine of their theology be contained by the wineskins of Judaism. This was because their christological pilgrimage led them far beyond the comprehension of Judaism. Jesus of Nazareth, as Risen Lord, was the new Temple, the goal of their journey, the place of the final Passover.

Jesus opened his mission with the proclamation: 'The rule of God is at hand' (Mark); 'The poor have the good news preached to them' (Luke)—amounting to the same thing. He had issued a call to *metanoia:* he had come to renew Israel. His ministry brought growth in his understanding of the Father's purpose: 'he learned obedience through what he suffered' (Heb 5:8). He found himself, at the end, face to face with the stark reality of the cross: '... not what I will, but what you will' (Mk 14:36). His was a pilgrimage of faith, of trust in the Father despite a gnawing sense of failure. He journeyed throughout the land of Israel: an itinerant prophet, with no home of his own. His last journey to Jerusalem marked him as indeed 'the pioneer and perfecter of our faith' (Heb 12:2). That journey to the cross stands as a challenge to his disciples. The cross was not the end of Jesus' journey; resurrection was inherent in his faithful death. His resurrection is our assurance that, beyond our death, we shall enter into his rest.

Spirituality
A grieving God had decided to blot out a humankind turned

hopelessly corrupt. He would not follow through, fully, on his threat: 'Noah found favour in the eyes of the Lord' (Gen 6:8). There is no doubt as to his stature: 'Noah was a righteous man, blameless in his generation' (6:9). He hearkened to the word of the Lord and acted on it without hesitation. He became recipient of a covenant, a covenant sealed not only with him but with all living creatures: the Lord will never again unleash a destructive flood on a world still going astray. Abraham is another paragon of virtue—*the* man of faith. At the Lord's bidding he got up and went, he knew not where. Though old and childless, 'in hope he believed against hope, that he should become the father of many nations' (Rom 4:18). He was ready—with a heavy heart—to sacrifice the child of promise. It is not so surprising, then, that Yahweh should want to disclose to this remarkable man his design for the wicked citizens of Sodom and Gomorrah (Gen 18:16-33). It is as though he had sought Abraham's approval! Jacob was unprincipled and did not hesitate to use people. All the more remarkable, then, his startling conversion. One can pinpoint the moment: his wrestling with God (32:22-31). He had wrestled in the darkness of night; afterwards 'the sun shone upon him' (v.31). Not just had his name been changed (Jacob to Israel): He was a radically changed man. We find him bowing humbly before Esau. The two were reconciled; for the first time Esau calls him 'brother' (33:1-11). We behold an older Jacob weeping for his lost son and, at the end, rejoicing: 'this my son was lost and is found'.

If Moses, at the start, was a reluctant deliverer, he grew in stature with the task. It was no light task, leading and caring for the people of Yahweh, a troublesome and fickle people. Moses made no bones about the weight of the burden nor about God's unfairness in, seemingly, expecting him to cope singlehanded. But he got on with the job. The verdict on this sterling man stands firm. God communicates with other prophets in visions and dreams—"Not so with my servant Moses. . . . With him I speak mouth to mouth clearly, and not in dark speech' (Num 12:6-8). No wonder that the deutero-nomist writes in his obituary: 'There has not arisen a prophet since like Moses, whom the Lord knew face to face' (Dt 34:10). God had spoken to Moses at the burning bush and Moses had come to know him truly.

Not so Jephthah. Here was a man of rude faith with an image of God to match. He sincerely believed that the favour of his God could be bought with human sacrifice, albeit in a critical situation. When it turned out that the designated victim was his only, much-loved, daughter he did not flinch: 'I have opened my mouth to the Lord, and I cannot take back my vow' (Jg 11:35). Jephthah's resolution is heroic. But he was a tragic victim of a false understanding of God. That magnanimous God, we may be sure, looked to the good faith of the one who had erred. Samson may have been a Nazarite dedicated to God (by his parents) but he was no 'man of God'. He is a comic figure in contrast to the tragic Jephthah. His earthy story reminds us that God has a sense of humour—and religion can do with a dash of humour. The idyll of Ruth strikes a charming note. The two women display mutual concerned love. If Ruth will not abandon her mother-in-law, Naomi works for the welfare of her dauther-in-law. And the worthy Boaz becomes the means of blessing on them both. All three lived, with simple directness, their faith in a gracious God.

David is a complex character. He could be magnanimous, but showed a cruel streak at times. What is not in question is his devotion to his God: 'he sang praise with all his heart, and he loved his Maker' (Sirach 47:8). There is the evocative image of a king who 'danced before the Lord with all his might' (2 Sam 6:14). David was human and could fall for a beautiful woman—even the wife of another. His infatuation drove him to murder. When challenged by a prophet he made no excuse: 'I have sinned against the Lord' (12:13). He could rise from his sin. Sinner and saint—a bit of both; and ever a sincere servant of his God. Amos was a man who thirsted for justice. He was merciless critic of a religion that served but to comfort the powerful. If his God seemed a stern judge and his message one of gloom, that may be fruit of the prophet's righteous anger. He was sure that his God would not tolerate exploitation and oppression. Amos was stirred to passion in his concern for the liberation of the oppressed.

Hosea had seen another side of God—a perception that was fruit of deep spiritual experience. He had discovered that love is the key that unlocks the secret of God. He had known the pain of love, the agony of faithfulness in face of infidelity. That experience won him an insight into the love of God. Hosea was a mystic. Among the Isaiahs, I shall settle for Second Isaiah. There is his remarkable optimism, flowing from indomitable faith. The Suffering Servant poems reveal something of the man; the mysterious Servant may well be the prophet himself. The religious figure who emerges is a fearless champion of justice who spurns strong-arm tactics: he will not break a bruised reed nor quench a smouldering wick (Is 42:1-4). Summoned to the task of winning back Israel he finds his strength only in God (49:1-6). Always alert to the word of the Lord, he will not he turned aside by painful opposition, serene in his knowledge that the Lord is his help (50:4-9). Though despised and rejected, he manfully bears the burden of human sorrow and human sin and offers himself for the salvation of his oppressors. Nothing other than a deep spiritual experience can account for that awesome portrait of heroic sanctity. Christians were quick to discover there the lineaments of Jesus.

Jeremiah is a more evocative parallel—for Jeremiah had walked to his Calvary. He knew his God and could, and did, dialogue with him. He made no secret of the fact that he did not enjoy his role of prophet of woe. Refreshingly, he complained loudly; but he stuck tirelessly, at risk to his life, with a hopeless mission. And when the long-threatened disaster struck he promptly became the consoler of his shattered people and spoke a message of hope. Faith in a God whom he knew to be a caring God had sustained Jeremiah. Faith in the real God is the only source of wholesome spirituality. Ezekiel managed to combine two spiritualities: those of prophet and priest. As prophet, he was much in the mould of Jeremiah. But where the latter had looked to a knowledge of God deep within the heart, and longed for a time when the externals of religion would scarcely matter (Jer 31:31-4), Ezekiel dreamt of a restored Temple and an ordered cult (Ezek 40:44). His was a spirituality largely nurtured by a liturgy. What of Jonah: a figure of satire, begrudger of God's mercy? He, rather like Jephthah, stands as warning. An unhealthy spirituality inevitably follows on a false perception of God.

Job had learned, through painful experience, that the received theology, which had served him up to now, no longer

162

met his case. The doctrine of retribution did not work in practice; and there could be suffering that did not flow from sin. More agonising than his attempt to cope with these problems was the absence of God. Job keeps crying out to a God who will not answer—even summoning that God to court. His experience is a classic instance of the 'dark night of the soul' described by later mystics. God had not withdrawn; but Job *felt* that he had. In reality he was, in his search, growing closer all the time to that hidden God. His situation shouted that God was uncaring—callous even. Job's sturdy faith will not accept that to be so. Nor will Qoheleth take that easier course because he, too, knows it to be false. More stringently than Job he stresses the theistic problem raised by the finality of death. Where is divine justice if *all* end up, without distinction, in Sheol? Qoheleth is the persistent questioner, but he questions on the basis of his faith. He anticipates the demand of 1 Peter 'to account for the hope that is in you' (3:14). The formidable faith of Job and Qoheleth, given their conviction that life effectively ended at death, is a challenge to Christians. It sets a question-mark against *our* faith.

Prayers of Esther, Judith and Tobit will offer us an insight into their spirituality. Before taking the fateful step of approaching the king uninvited—thereby risking her life—Esther, 'seized with deathly anxiety, fled to the Lord' (14:1). She protests that her royal station is not of her choosing. She has no joy in being queen; her only joy is in the Lord. She ends her prayer with the plea: 'And save me from my fear!' (14:19). Her sole hope is in the help of her God. Before embarking on her heroic venture Judith, too, turned to the Lord. Already we know that she had spent the years of her widowhood in prayer and fasting and in meticulous observance of Torah. She times her prayer, now, to coincide with the evening offer of incense in the Jerusalem temple (9:1). Perhaps nowhere else than in the conclusion of the prayer is the faithful Israelite's sense of total dependence on God so forcefully expressed. As for Tobit; he, like Judith, was a wholehearted observer of Torah and practised, assiduously, the traditional good works of almsgiving, prayer and fasting. His spirituality is not for himself but is outward-looking. In his 'prayer of rejoicing' (ch. 13) he declares:

I give him thanks in the land of my captivity,
and I show his power and majesty to a nation of sinners
(v. 6).

John the Baptist had all the uncompromising directness of
Amos. It is not surprising that he brought upon himself the
hatred of Herodias: no woman likes to be publicly proclaimed
a harlot. Intriguing is the ambivalent attitude of Antipas:
'Herod feared John, knowing that he was a righteous and holy
man.... When he heard him, he was much perplexed; and yet
he heard him gladly' (Mk 6:20). It says so much about the
compelling religious stature of John. If Mary of Nazareth is
handmaid of the Lord, that does not mark her as a passive
figure. Her very role—'mother of my Lord'—speaks elo-
quently of her spiritual calibre. Her ready response to what she
had spontaneously recognised as a call of her God presupposes
a life of close communion with that God. She was to learn that
communion with God and utter faithfulness to his ways would
not spare her from a sword of shared pain. Mary of
Nazareth—despite her unique role—was matched by another
Mary for openness to the Lord and generous love. While
identification of Mary Magdalene with the anonymous woman
of Luke 7 is out of the question, we may be sure that the one
healed by Jesus of a severe mental illness (that is what is meant
by the phrase, 'from whom seven demons had gone out', Lk
8:2) would not have been remiss in showing her gratitude. Her
discipleship of Jesus prepared her for her role of proclaimer of
the resurrection. She, too, was a woman of great faith.
We admire the unselfish person. To be ready to
acknowledge the talents of others and to be happy to live in
their shadow, calls for maturity. Only a solid spiritual base
could have supported Barnabas on his magnanimous way. He
accepted, with humility, that the Saul he had fostered was
greater than he. For Paul love of Christ was the mainspring of
his life: caritas Christi urget nos. That love sustained him in the
trials of his missionary ventures, the frustrating factor of
troublesome disciples, the bitter opposition of fellow-
Christians. Through Jesus of Nazareth he had come to know
better his Hebrew God; a God wholly for us (Rom 8:31-9). As
one who had, formerly, sought the support of Torah, he would

now boast of his weakness, his total dependence on God: 'My grace is sufficient for you, for my power is made perfect in weakness' (2 Cor 12:9).

A man who could see with the clarity of Mark had to have a direct line to God. He had come to terms with the death of Jesus and earnestly wanted his community to do the same. His appreciation of the suffering of Jesus—witness his Gethsemane scene and the cry from the cross—surely had come from personal experience of suffering. He, too, must have cried out: 'my God, my God, why have you forsaken me?' He, too, must have known the dark night of Job. Luke's spirituality was more tranquil; he was enthralled by the gentleness of Jesus. And he embraced that loving, forgiving Father of Jesus. His sensitive spirit responded to Jesus' concern for the poor. His perception is summed-up in the declaration of the Lord: 'The Son of man came to seek and save the lost' (Lk 19:10).

The confident faith of the author of Hebrews shines through his letter; he *knows* that he will attain his rest. And all because his thoroughly human High Priest has assured him, beyond doubt, that God is a God bent on the salvation of humankind. From the depth of his faith he urges: 'Let us with confidence draw near to the throne of grace' (4:16). And again: 'Let us draw near with a true heart in full assurance of faith' (10:22). Ought not such be the calm assurance of the Christian? If we step behind the Johannine community to the chief architect of the Fourth Gospel we find a matching tranquillity. It is epitomised in the allegory of the vine (Jn 15:1-11). Johannine spirituality flows from union with Jesus: 'I am the true vine . . . you are the branches'. It follows that 'without me you can do nothing'. Faithful abiding in Jesus is not alone source of lived spirituality ('he who abides in me . . . bears much fruit') it has to be ground of deep and lasting peace.

'Be imitators of me, as I am of Christ' (1 Cor 11:1). Paul's way was an *imitatio Christi.* Though Paul, in his letters, has little or nothing to say of the life of Jesus of Nazareth, we have good reason to believe that he knew very well the pattern of Jesus' life. It may be, for instance, that the heart of his hymn to love (1 Cor 13) is based on the life-style and conduct of Jesus (cf. 13:4-7). What was the secret of Jesus' own life of total loving service? Jesus was one who had a serene relationship with God. Without self-consciousness he spoke of 'Father' and 'Son'; he turned with direct confidence to that Father in prayer. The gospel evidence points to Jesus' consistent use of *Abba*—a familiar designation of one's earthly parent—in speaking of God and especially in prayer to God. The practice shows his unconventional regard towards God and his sense of intimate communion with him. We seek and find the ground of Jesus' Abba-experience in his humanness—in a humanness always directly related to God. In Jesus of Nazareth God had met his counterpart, the image and likeness of himself. To Jesus he could say, 'My Son' and hear the spontaneous reply 'Abba'. The way of Jesus has made clear to us that God is to be found in humanness. He is, in truth, *our* God-for-us.

A mixed bag indeed, those men and women—all, in their measure, servants of God; and they are but a few of a goodly number. In their variety we discern two constant features. Their God is ever the Father of our Lord Jesus Christ—he is immediately recognisable as such in Hosea, Jeremiah and Job for instance. And there is, each time, a suggestion at least of pilgrimage; it may be a journey of faith. Heroes and heroines, servants of the one God: we can learn from them, from their lives—their pilgrim spirituality. 'Since we are surrounded by so great a cloud of witnesses... let us run with perseverance the race that is set before us' (Heb 12:1).

EXCURSUS

Biblical Spirituality: An Irish Dimension
SEÁN DE PAOR

Molaimis anois daoine cháiliúla, na sinsir ... (Sir 44)

When Jesus ben Sirach made this roll-call of 'famous ancestors' he was doing something which the human heart gladly responds to, and that for two reasons—the fame and the family pride. But he was interested above all in a third thing: religion. The word he used for this was *hesed*[1]—rendered well enough by 'pious' or 'faithful'. Sirach was a wisdom-teacher. He was at once traditional and creative—not an easy achievement in any age. His influence on the New Testament is not inconsiderable. Much as I would like to, I am not going to trace his influence on the Irish tradition but simply suggest that his roll-call technique was something the Irish also developed in their litany tradition.

The focus, then, is on religion; or, as Sirach puts it at the close of his work: 'Blessed is the one who has a concern for these things ... whoever does them will be strong in every way, for the light of the Lord is his path' (Sir 50:28-9). Reflecting on God and living with God: such is wisdom. It can be a very lonely matter so we need the comfort of those who walk the same path; we need fellow-pilgrims. When our teachers are fellow-pilgrims they are all the more appealing and all the more convincing. We gladly turn to models of spirituality, or spiritual people, the saints—including those who are not officially 'canonised'. In somewhat the same way as our age might be summed up in a phrase like 'the medium is the message', one could sum up the gospel in the phrase 'the human is divine'. We are going to look at some Irish Christian wayfarers—flesh of our flesh and children of our land.

Not So Long Ago...

Mícheál Ó Guithín, the poet son of Peig Sayers of the Blaskets, who had written her own story, in Irish, begins his Preface to this autobiographical account: 'Praise be the King of creation, but it was little I thought the dear old grey head of my mother contained things of such import . . .'.[2] Peig's reflections could on occasion be tiresome, but what she describes as 'the good things and the bad' which she had lived through corresponds closely enough to our own experience. In fact, she had more than her enough of bad things. Have we ever reflected how she coped, or what gave her the strength to survive such trials? Her road was not rose-petalled; her spirituality was robust. To call her a saint might only obscure the issue.

An incident recounted by Robin Flower[3]—an English pilgrim who has adequately repaid the hospitality shown him on the Blaskets—concerning Tomás Ó Criomhthain sheds further light on our path, and incidentally tells us much about God. His God and our God? One day, on Robin's return from London, Tomás presented him with a fish. He began to thank Tomás in his 'halting Irish'. 'Don't thank me till you've heard all my story,' he says. 'Well,' I say, 'no story could make any difference to my thanks.' 'Listen then. When I came back from fishing this morning I had two bream, one large and one smaller. The one there is not the larger of the two.' 'How comes that?' I say, smelling a jest in the wind. 'Well, it was this way. I came into my house and I laid the two fish down on the table, and I said to myself: 'now which of these two fish shall I give the gentleman from London?' And there came into my head the old saying, 'when the Lord made Heaven and Earth at the first, he kept the better of the two for himself'. And where could I find a higher example?' The black and white beauty of these characters delights us. And rightly so, for they are bone of our bone. Can it be true that 'their likes will not be, ever again'?

Long, Long Ago . . . Patrick

'The stone that lay in the mud is now at the top of the wall' (*Conf.* 12).

When the world was considerably younger but yet quite old already, Jesus of Nazareth came to Ireland. The Irish welcomed Jesus and with little ado became Christians. Patrick was the divinely-inspired mediator of this new departure. But Patrick was not the first Irish Christian. Indeed he was not Irish but, more than likely, a Welshman. Apart from that, there were already Christians in Ireland before Patrick came along. These seem to have been in the Leinster area.[4]

We know most about Patrick from his own writings—his *Confession* and his *Letter to Coroticus*. These are spiritual and personal rather than historical reports. For our present purpose they are ideal. The man we see here is human and noble, vulnerable and magnanimous, passionate yet detached, largely self-made yet humble and ready to let God have all the glory. He has suffered and laboured, he has given his life for the cause he believes in, for the God whom he loves and for the people whom willy-nilly he calls his own. He was an exile and was very conscious of the fact that this was to be a life sentence—he would never see his home again. All this must, however, be seen in the light of the great joy with which he accepts the angelic call to begin his mission.

Patrick wrote his *Confession* near the close of his life. This seems to have been a source of regret to him; but 'What good is an excuse?' he asks.[5] The very title *confessio* bespeaks his sense of the Bible—even though he may have heard of or read Augustine's *Confessions*. For instance, he writes: 'it is right to reveal and publish the works of God' (Tob 12:7).[6] His faith and his sense of the presence of God are probably the most striking elements in Patrick's theology. It is not hard to see shining through his words the figures of Abraham—faith and devotion to God; Moses—leadership of a bondage people out of the darkness of exile, and his lawgiving; David—his being a prophet and psalmsinger. And so on, up to his resemblance to Paul and indeed to Christ—especially in so far as he was persecuted and had to defend his motives and intentions. In this he takes Paul's Second Corinthians as his model.[7]

Later traditions were not slow to exploit these elements. While one such tradition has him go to Rome[8] to receive his commission, another has him go to Sinai! His fast is that of Moses, Elijah and Jesus. His tending sheep/swine makes him a Moses or a David; his baptism of the Irish recalls Moses and the water from the rock. (In the later Middle Ages, Christ Church, Dublin possessed part of the Mosaic table of the Law—no doubt brought back from Sinai by Patrick!)[9]

Patrick saw himself as the apostle of the Irish, 'at the ends of the earth'—indeed as the last of the Apostles: a fisher and a hunter for the increase of his Lord's household. Many dangers and difficulties beset him in this task but he had a shield in the presence of his new God, Christ the Lord. This is what the eighth-century 'Breastplate' (attributed to him) has him celebrate. It certainly shows an unerring sense of the theology of Patrick, and of the native Celtic theology also in so far as such incantations or charms were the stock-in-trade of his main opponents, the Druids. Yet it is true that 'what little is known of early Irish paganism strongly suggests that it was unlikely to put up a forceful resistance to the preaching of Christianity'.[10]

The deep loneliness, isolation and sense of opposition and rejection felt by Patrick could have made him a bitter man or at best a self-pitying bore. But no. His basic nobility and his ability to see his own weaknesses made him gratefully content and happily detached. His energy and his undoubted success, coupled with this pain and human hurt, and combined with his sense of God and his prayer, make him the model pilgrim. His heart is in his heavenly homeland but there is a task to be done in the meantime here below. He is on the dusty tiring road, but that is all the while being left behind.

With typical Celtic imagination the historical Patrick has often been seen mythologically. Yet, if we try a little, we can read through the myths and be nourished on the marrow. We can find the divine in the human. Patrick, using the Bible myth, saw himself as a stranger and pilgrim during his exile and so gave a base to the Irish pilgrimage and missionary élan. We should never forget that his knowledge of the Irish language, religion and social customs and organisation gained him his leadership position. And this, coupled with the new Latin Christianity, learning and religion, is the recipe that gives us an Irish Church. In any age this remains the recipe; but if we want fresh bread there must be a new baking.

It is paradoxical that Patrick's popularity has tended to make him less well known. For instance, his *Confession* is not often read—except perhaps for his feast day. It is such a strikingly strong biblical document that one expects more to be made of it. The early Irish, on the other hand, had such a respect for him that they never used his name as a personal name, but would call themselves 'Gilla'—or 'Máel Pátraic' (servant of Patrick). It was only with the Anglo-Normans that the name came into current use.[11] In the seventh century his feast was a three-day affair, when his hymn *Audite omnes*[12]—by Colmán Elo—was sung and three Homilies preached. Any attempt at an elaboration of an Irish theology has to begin with an attentive listening to Patrick.

Most of the theological works of the early Irish Church are anonymous. They must be read in conjunction with the *Lives* of the saints in order to put flesh on them and personalise them. On the whole, these *Lives* are later, from the tenth century on, but because they are not meant as biographies they can easily be used to fill out the social and cultural-theological atmosphere of pre-Norman Ireland. This was by no means a Golden Age. In fact, it was an age when gold was often more sought after than God or religion. Besides, the notion of a Golden Age is itself a myth, a pagan myth. Even if the human becomes the 'all too human' it is still where the God of the Christians is to be found. The very idea of pilgrimage, and the pilgrim Church, is rather the correlative of the 'all too human' and not of a Golden Age. Christianity is what happens when an individual or a people meets Christ and lives out the new relationship according to the peculiar genius of each. There is no real blueprint or goldenprint, only examples of the Gospel and the Living Spirit to produce the new baking.

Brighid

'Power went out from her and healed all . . .'.

In many ways Brighid is a female Patrick. Even what we said about the use of the personal name in his case is paralleled by Gilla—,Máel-Brigte (ending up today as MacBride). Very little is known about the historical Brighid, except that she lived into the sixth century. Some would count up to six *Lives* of her and they all agree as to her stature and importance. For some indeed this importance was political, but this might be seen as an indication of her reality. In the seventh century, when *Lives* of her began to be written, there was already a widespread cult of Brighid in place. This was, it seems clear, grafted on to a strong pagan goddess's cult. Gerald Barry (of Wales), that ambitious and somewaht sour twelfth-century bishop, whose account of Ireland makes fascinating reading, speaks of the perpetual fire of Kildare.[13] R.A.S. Macalister, writing in 1919, speaks of this fire as the focus of a college of priestesses at whose head was none other than Brighid.[14] Her conversion and the transformation of Kildare into a Christian monastery he sees as the greatest of her miracles.

Propagandist though he may be, it is to Cogitosus[15] we now turn for a sketch of Brighid's personality. A key tenet of his is the power (*virtus*) of Brighid. He begins, however, with a description of her as 'beautiful in character and welcoming (*hospitalis*)'. This, I suggest, gives a gentler direction to the essentially male notion of power. There may, after all, have been a deeper reason for the apparent equality of Brighid and Patrick as 'the pillars of the Irish, of one heart and mind'.[16] Indeed, quite a few of her miracles were in the service of the poor, the strangers and pilgrims. Her first was when the butter of her mother's dairy, which she had given away to the poor, was miraculously replaced by God at her request. Furthermore, her prayer to God on that occasion was powered by the 'strongly burning inextinguishable fire of faith'.[17] We note the evocation of the pagan fire. And faith is spoken of in a whole cluster of Gospel terms and promises: 'All things are possible to believers; The works I do, you also . . . ; You are the light of the world . . . ; have faith like a grain of mustard'.[18] A similar juxtaposition of the pagan and the Christian is found later—in the story of the millstone which will not grind the corn of a pagan (*paganus, magus, gentilis*), even when he has secretly got another man to bring the corn. Nor will fire burn this stone; and this same stone is later placed near Brighid's church as a healing stone.[19]

Cogitosus, alias Toimtenach speaks much of his heroine as an itinerant preacher.[20] She travelled about in her chariot like a bishop (*pontifice*),[21] preaching, and confirming her doctrine by miracles.[22] In this she is like Christ, serene and happy, and wanting all to be saved. She went about doing good: in this she is obviously like Jesus but also like her 'patronymic' who was daughter of the Dagda—that is, the 'good god'. Thus she was a pilgrim; and many people flocked to her as pilgrims. They saw her 'city' as a place of sanctuary. Some came for food, some for healing, some out of curiosity, and some to bring gifts.[23] The latter reason is not the most Christian and should warn us about the danger of power in that it attracts wealth. Patrick's insistence on poverty and his refusal of gifts will always remain a serious challenge to the 'too' human in every Christian.

The pilgrim aspect of the Brighid tradition is illustrated by a story in the Lismore *Life* which epitomises that sense of urgency which compelled the Celtic practice of pilgrimage: 'Brighid was once with her sheep on the Curragh and she saw running past her a son of reading (that is, a student—of the Bible), Nindid. 'What makes you move, O son of reading', says Brighid, 'and what seek you in that wise?' 'O nun,' says the scholar, 'I am going to heaven.' 'The Virgin's Son knows', says Brighid, that happy is the one who goes that journey, and for God's sake pray for me that it may be easy for me to go.' 'O nun,' says he, "I have no leisure, for the gates of heaven are open now and I fear they may be shut against me..."'[24] Here Brighid is shown to be in complete harmony with the pilgrim. She later saved from poisoning three scholars of her household on their way to Rome. And Nindid came from Rome to give her the last rites.

So we come to the death of Brighid, around 520. As Cogitosus puts it: she 'cast off the body' (just as she had hung her wet cloak on a sunbeam!) 'and followed the Lamb into the heavenly mansions.'[25] This is the same lady he had so often shown as minding her sheep or her cows or her pigs. In fact another aspect of her power is her control over the brute creation: an anticipated paradise, or paradise regained. Let us end by evoking a further evergreen legend about Brighid. Gerald of Wales tells of 'Brighid's pastures' that no one dared plough.[26] (This is probably another form of Cogitosus' story of the wooden altar-base breaking into new growth at the virgin's touch.) And though all the animals of the province ate the grass of the pasture, when morning came it was as plentiful as ever! This recalls the manna story of the book of Exodus.

Coemgen (Beautiful Child)
'When his mother saw what a fair child he was...' (Ex 2:2).
Kevin of Glendalough, who died around 618, is not noted for meekness but rather for having got rid of an importunate woman by dumping her into the lake! And yet his very name

seems to point to Moses, the meekest of men. Reading the longest Latin *Life,* one sees that there is a basis for this comparision with Moses and quite a basis for his attitude towards women. Like Jesus he was refused baptism (cf. Mt 3:14)—because, in his case, an angel had already performed the rite. A mysterious white cow supplied milk for this fine child.[27] Given the frequent appearance of cows in the story, and seeing that the cow was pretty much the hub of the economy, we may simply take it that Kevin was quite at home in this world; he was no misfit.

As a youth he had beaten off, with nettles, his first temptress—quenching one fire with another. She repented, and became a nun. Nor does physical fire burn him, as the following story (in the *Life*) tells us. Like Brighid, he loved the poor and pilgrims. Once, he gave away all the meat and beer prepared for the farm workers but then, Cana-wise, went on to supply enough new meat and wine for a three-day feast.[28]

The wild beasts befriended him in his lonely hermitage and drank water from his hand.[29] Brandubh, out hunting one day, came upon the praying saint surrounded by playing animals and singing birds. Even the leaves and branches of the trees sang to him to sweeten his labours.[30] He once met a hungry she-wolf and permitted her to eat a cow's new calf. But the misery of the cow touched his heart and he pleaded with the wolf to act as her calf and console her until she had a new calf.[31]

The devils met frustration upon frustration in face of his toughness and rigid self-discipline. They were even forced to look for sympathy from Comhgall (another saint) after the failure of an all-out seven-year assault. The only weak point they could find was his constant longing to go on pilgrimage—evil in the guise of good. But even here they failed. On one occasion Munna[32] warned Kevin that it was the devil's idea. Another time he had got as far as Dublin when Garbán[33] of Cenn Sáile near Swords put him back on the rails. On the way home he called to see Berchán[34] This same Berchán was himself once severely tempted by a woman; the whole scene being viewed from afar by Kevin and Crónán.[35] When Berchán began to beat her off with his staff, Crónán cheered him on, but Kevin restrained him. The woman was duly impressed and did not even have to become a nun.

The final incident I cite is the rather long account of his foster-child Faelán.[36] A certain Colmán had divorced his wife. In revenge, she resolved to put a curse on any child born of the new wife. The couple did eventually manage to get a baby baptised and safely off to Kevin for sanctuary before any spells could work. This child was Faelán. In the end the woman located the boy, now well grown (reared on doe's milk), and she came to curse him from the hill facing the monastery. Kevin prayed. She was struck blind and fell to her death in the lake. Is this the true version of the story of the temptress most often associated with Kevin?

To the angel-planner[37] of Glendalough's future wealth and glory who offered to remove the mountains, Kevin replied: 'I do not desire to remove God's creatures for my sake, and anyhow all the wild beasts are homely and humble with me, and this would sadden them. . . . God can help me some other how.' Again we get a hint about the ambiguity of wealth and glory.

Kevin is also made to meet many of the important figures of his stature—if not of his own time: Columba, Cainneach, Comhgall, Kieran (Clonmacnoise) and so on.[38] And he is three times[39] described as singing the hymn of Patrick—'the Archbishop who converted Ireland from paganism to the Faith . . .'.

The Age of Peregrinatio[40]

'Wanderers . . . of whom the world was not worthy' (Heb 11:38).

The Irish Church has always been a pilgrim Church, but there have been different periods and emphases. A watershed seems to have coincided with the influence of Bede in the 730s. He admired the Irish and spoke highly of their hospitality to many English exiles and pilgrim students. But the Easter controversy seemed to him to have shown up the Irish as not a little odd. They had better be left to their own devices; they were certainly not to be imitated. Their influence on Europe was henceforth to be counterbalanced by the Anglo-Saxon-Carolingian-Benedictine axis. This, at any rate, seems to be how things turned out. Order, tidiness and growing sophistication ruled out wandering individualists, however holy. The Irish had regarded pilgrimage as, among other things, a penance-punishment—so, inevitably, some undesirables might be encountered on the roads of Europe. From now on, only the deeper valid motives could prevail, and even then the tendency would be to interiorise the journey, to spiritualise the quest. With the Viking presence the hardship motive could only be more marked and many anchorites, heirs of the seventh-century pilgrims, would achieve the longed-for goal of martyrdom. Patrick had already spoken of his readiness for martyrdom.[41]

In the ninth century many still wandered, but more as simple exiles and scholars than as holy pilgrims and preachers. Indeed the tenth century would see the watershed affect even the scholarly scene with certain turning-points in exegesis.[42] Another avenue which the pilgrim urge had taken in the eighth century was the Voyage, whether real or, more likely, of fantasy. Hence we have the *Brendan Voyage(s)* and a host of others. We should always remember that we are here dealing with literature, with a desire for entertainment and delight in a good story. We might just as well ask the location of Tír na nÓg, for its story and theirs are of the same cloth. The real tenth and eleventh century pilgrims went to a particular destination, mostly Rome. In this the Irish were drawing nearer to the Catholic norm.

As an example of the underlying spirituality let us look at a litany of *circa* 800, probably from Lismore.[42a] It has a list of pilgrim saints. It offers a vivid illustration of the Irish conception of pilgrimage. Its content is unusual for it is peopled by Roman pilgrims and Egyptian monks as well as by Britons, Saxons, Galls and Irish. In the mid-seventh century Lismore had a flourishing school of biblical and theological studies within whose orbit such a work as *De Mirabilibus Sacrae Scripturae*[43] was written in 655. Apart from the fact that saints with Lismore links are prominent in the afore-mentioned litany, its catholic sweep also fits this early Irish university which was renowned for its litanies. The term 'Roman' here may have been used in the sense of the 'saying' of Patrick: '...the church of the Irish, nay more of the Romans'. The term had earlier taken on a more pointed meaning in the now defunct Easter controversy. Celtic and Roman traditions can now happily co-exist and coracles of Roman pilgrims alternate with Celtic voyagers to the western seas in search of the Land of Promise. The age-old Celtic urge to go beyond can be accommodated with a little imagination, a sense of humour and wonder.

A few of the invocations of this Litany will give us a glimpse into the mind of a ninth-century disciple of Mochuta of Lismore.

1. Thrice fifty coracles of Roman pilgrims who landed in Erin with Elias, Natalis, etc.

Hos omnes invoco per Iesum.

2. Three thousand authorities who assembled from Munster for one quest with bishop Ibar, to whom the angels brought the great feast which Brighid made to Jesus in her heart.

Hos omnes...

St Ibar (or Ibor) is closely connected with Brighid in written sources and it is he who spoke of her as 'Mary of the Gael'. As we saw above, Brighid was noted for hospitality to the poor and to pilgrims. A poem attributed to Brighid has her say: 'I should like a great lake of ale for the King of kings, I should like the household of heaven to be drinking it for eternity'.

3. Thrice fifty men of orders, true royal heroes every one of them, of the Gaels, who went in one company on pilgrimage with Abban Mac hUí Chormaic

Hos omnes...

4. Thrice fifty other pilgrims who went with Abban to Erin of men of Rome and Latium

Hos omnes...

Abban was the nephew of Ibar and had special powers over the sea so that if one going to sea recited thrice the couplet: 'The curragh of Abban on the water/And the fair company of Abban within it', one returned safe.

11. Thrice fifty true pilgrims across the sea with Buite the bishop, and ten holy virgins.

Hos omnes...

Buite is the Boice of Monasterboice.

12. The twelve pilgrims who went with Medoc of Ferns across the sea.

Hos omnes...

The *Life* of Medoc has much of seafaring.

16.   Three score men who went with Brendan to seek the Land of Promise.

Hos omnes...

18.   Four and twenty men of Munster who went with Ailbe on the ocean to revisit the Land of Promise, who are alive there till doom. And [as another text says] have no light save the sunny countenance of one towards the other.

Hos omnes...

19.   The anchorite whom Brendan found before him in the Land of Promise, with all the saints who fell in the islands of the ocean. [Another text adds] i.e. the household of Patrick.

Hos omnes...

Columba (*c* 521-97).

'Leave your own land, and your people ... (Gen 12:1).

The ninth-tenth century *Life of Columba* in the Book of Lismore[44] has him in contact with Brighid at Swords. Though their lives may have slightly overlapped they are unlikely to have met. There is a famous saying uttered in advice by the Abbess Samthan (+739) at her abbey of Clonbroney near Granard to a male seeker of spiritual direction that 'since God is near to all who call upon him no necessity is laid on us to cross the sea, for one can approach the kingdom of God from any land'. This same idea recurs in another form in the *Life* of Columba: 'For it is not by footsteps, nor by motion of body, that one draws nigh to God, but by practising virtue and good deeds.'[45] This *Life* is basically a homily and the main part of it is a commentary on Gen 12:1—'*Exi de terra ...*'. It is, in effect, a treatise on pilgrimage and, in light of what I have sketched as the history of the idea, it is of special interest. Here is the gist of it.

Faith is what the story of Abraham is all about. The Lord himself gave this friendly gracious counsel to him: '*Exi...*'. It has come down to us in the Church through Moses, the leader of God's people who wrote Genesis, so that Paul can say that those who believe are sons of Abraham. For the sake of the Lord of the Elements the sons must follow their faithful father and leave all and go as pilgrims into the Land of Promise. The message comes to us in three ways: by the example of the saints such as Paul and Anthony of Egypt; by preachers of the divine Scripture after the example of Paul's preaching; and finally by tribulations after the example of the people of Israel who turned to the Lord from their sojourn in the land of idols and troubles.

There are three ways in which the message may summon us to knowledge of the Lord and membership of his family (*muinnterus*),[46] and three ways we may leave the homeland. First, in the body only, a pilgrimage which does not sever from sin and vices, and it is labour in vain. For it was only after Abraham had left in body that the word came, saying: '*Exi de terra* . . .'. Only virtue and good deeds draw one nigh to God. A second way leaves the homeland in desire of heart and mind but not in body; it is the way of those who minister as clergy. Thirdly, one may leave in body and soul as the Apostle did, and those of the perfect pilgrimage for whom the Lord foretold great good (cf. Mt 19:29). The prophet speaks of these when he says: 'I give thee thanks for it, O God, I am a pilgrim and exile like my fathers' (Ps 38:13).

This third and perfect way was followed by a multitude in the Old and New Testaments. And Columba took that path, he 'the high saint, the high sage and the son chosen by God, the archpresbyter of the Gael and the brand of battle of the Holy Spirit . . . Columba son of Feidlimid'.[47] Such a vigorous and direct reading of the Gospel balances the tendency to interiorise which was current at that time. This seems to have been dictated mainly by the fact that the homilist was talking about Columba who lived in the sixth century and who certainly did go on pilgrimage in this manner and who did preach the gospel far and wide. So much is clear from the seventh-century Adomnan. Thus the Lismore life has Columba preach throughout all of Ireland before turning to Scotland. He looks like a Patrick *redivivus* and, sure enough, the *Life* has Patrick foretell his coming as 'a sage, a prophet, a poet, a lovable lamp, pure and clear . . .'.[47a]

The whole focus, then, is on faith, faith lived and preached.

179

There is nothing sectarian or interior or even monastic in his reading of the Bible. This Columba is being straightforwardly apostolic. He is said to have wanted to go to Rome or Jerusalem but got only as far as Tours, from where he brought back to Derry the Gospel of Martin. He was a learned man, especially in the Bible, and wrote 300 books—as well as building 300 churches! Always we notice the apostolic-faith aspect. Adomnan, in Chapter 18 of Book III of his Life, describes a three-day period of intense vision during which he sees 'openly revealed many of the secret things that have been hidden since the world began. Also all things that in the scriptures are dark and most difficult became plain and were shown more clearly than the day to the eyes of his purest heart'. Unfortunately, he says, Baithene was not there to write it all down.[48]

In Chapter 22 Columba says 'thirty years have been completed of my pilgrimage in Britain ... and I have besought the Lord to release me from my sojourn (*incolatus*) and at once call me to the heavenly country'. He speaks of the overwhelming joy he experiences at 'the calm and lovely sight of the holy angels which fills the heart of the elect with joy and exultation ... wonderful and incomparable ...'. But the angels have to wait a further five years 'beyond the strait of the island (Iona)', before the Lord will release him from his 'weary *peregrinatio*'.

Conclusion

'The one for whom little is not enough will not be satisfied by more.'[49] So might the formidable Columban have suggested to anyone who thinks that this small tour of the early Irish spirituals is all too little. The same harsh Columban was, however, capable of sending by post the forgotten kiss which last-minute haste had precluded![50] There is no disputing the stature of this man who dominated Europe in his time. But can we get nearer to him and listen to his heart? The letter from which I have just quoted has some flashes of tenderness: 'To his most sweet sons and dearest disciples'. 'For what advantage is it to have a body and not to have a heart?'[51] It also contains another recurring thought of his: 'We desire to know all, we tire of doing all we know, hoping that words can count instead of deeds... '[52] this is, in fact, one meaning of the initial saying: 'for whom little is not enough'. In Letter 6 he issues a reproach that his past teachings have not satisfied; but 'my dearest sons must be often taught and instructed, so that by some of the delights of letters they may be able to conquer their own griefs arising out of inner conflict'.[53] We 'tire of doing' because we are down, and we want to escape into reading or discussion or seeking more advice. This is why publishers can always sell more spiritual books!

Columban next uses this saying in relation to the Trinity.[54] Again his idea is that worlds and discussions do not supply for, but only dodge, acting out our beliefs. The Trinity is unsearchable and ineffable. Faith is a journey and we travel this road not by feet or words but by love. The 'little' thing that we can know and search out is the creation, so that we may get to know the Creator.[55]

The saying is also used in connection with contempt of the world.[56] If one does not discern this little thing that is the misery of the world, how can it be seen for what it is? If they will not listen to Moses, will they listen to one from the dead? We do not see because we do not want to. The little we have to be getting on with is faith. The idea is that if we really grasp the basics we are set up. As Lonergan says in his not so little book *Insight*: 'understand what it is to understand and... all knowledge is yours'.[57]

A final, and twofold, use of the same idea is found in the *Rules*.[58] In Rule 4 Columban is commenting on Cassian's threefold Renunciation. Our Poverty is against the vice of Greed. Our real needs are very few, in fact, only one thing is necessary—love, *pauca caritatis*. In Rule 8 he is treating of Discretion. We can achieve the balance of discretion if we pursue sufficiency.

In his first Sermon[59] Columban cites the saying as Scripture, whereas it is, in fact, from the writings of Sulpicius Severus (*Dial.* 1:18). The text he may have in mind is likely Exodus 16:17-18,21 dealing with the manna. It recurs also in 2 Corinthains 8:15. But the most interesting allusion is to the sufficiency which is at the heart of discretion. This is close to 1 Timothy 6. There, in 6:6, the idea developed is *autarkeia*, a Platonic idea which aims at self-sufficiency: not having to depend on more. This is a pagan notion developed in New Testament Christianity. It is close to the heart of the gospel in so far as what is at stake is freedom.

Life, then, for Columban, is a way,[60] a journey, a hard road. It is discipline;[61] it is knowing the goal[62] and knowing how best to reach it. Columban is a pilgrim, a man in a hurry, so he travels light—in fact with only the bare necessities as viaticum.[63] He had left what he calls 'the world's end, where spiritual leaders fight the Lord's battles'. He had hoped to see heroes but he finds 'corpses' and he suggests that the cause of all these evils is 'prosperity's ease'.[64]

At the close of our period another Irish pilgrim, possibly Sedulius Scottus, has this final, hard-earned, wryly-expressed, advice for the pilgrim—surely fruit of his own experience:

> Pilgrim, take care your journey's not in vain,
> a hazard without profit, without gain;
> the King you seek you'll find in Rome, it's true,
> but only if he travels on the way with you.[65]

NOTES

(1) The Yahwist is the conventional designation of the tenth-century BC author of an important strand of the Pentateuch—the Yahwistic tradition. The name derives from the fact that the author consistently uses the proper name 'Yahweh' of God.

The Priestly writers (priests of the Jerusalem Temple) account for much of the Pentateuch material, and gave its final form to the Pentateuch (probably fifth-century BC). The two strands that make up our existing Genesis flood-story display the distinctive styles and concerns of the Yahwistic and Priestly writings.

(2) See Claus Westermann, *Genesis 1-11. A Commentary*, London: SPCK 1986; Bernhard W. Anderson, 'From Analysis to Synthesis: The Interpretation of Genesis 1-11', *Journal of Biblical Literature* 97 (1978), 23-39.

(3) See Erich Zenger, 'Orthodoxy and Orthopraxis in the Old Testament', *Concilium*, No. 192, 1987, 12-13.

(4) See Helen Schüngel-Straumann, 'Gott als Mutter in Hosea 11', *Theologische Quartalschrift*, 166:2 (1986), 119-34.

(5) Aelred Cody, O.S.B., *Ezekiel*, Wilmington,DE: M.Glazier 1984, 254-5).

(6) Walter Brueggemann, 'A Shape for Old Testament Theology, I. Structure Legitimation; II. Embrace of Pain', *The Catholic Biblical Quarterly* 47 (1985), 28-46; 395-415; here page 400 is cited.

(7) See pp. 48-9.

(8) *The Gospel According to St John*, Vol. 1, London: Burns & Oates 1968, 216.

(9) Rudolf Schnackenburg, *The Gospel According to St John*, Vol. 3, New York: Crossroad 1982, 274-82.

(10) E.P. Sanders, *Paul, the Law and the Jewish People*, London: SCM 1983, 153.

(11) David Rhoads and Donald Michie, *Mark as Story*. An Introduction to the Narrative of a Gospel, Philadelphia: Fortress 1982, 115.

(12) See Richard J. Cassidy, *Society and Politics in the Acts of the Apostles*, Maryknoll, N.Y.: Orbis 1987.

(13) Hugh W. Montefiore, *The Epistle to the Hebrews*, London: A. & C. Black 1964, 85-6.

(14) See Raymond E. Brown, *The Epistles of John*, New York: Doubleday 1982; Jerome Neyrey, *Christ is Community: The Christologies of the New Testament*, Wilmington, DE: M. Glazier 1985.

(15) Edward Schillebeeckx, *Jesus in Our Western Culture. Mysticism, Ethics and Politics*, London: SCM 1987, 19-20.

(16) See Wilfrid Harrington, *Jesus and Paul. Signs of Contradiction*, Wilmington, DE: M. Glazier 1987, 73-90, 183-97.

Seán de Paor, 167-82.

1. Sir 43:33
2. Author's translation. The title 'King of Creation' (Rí na nDúl) recurs often in the Irish *Lives*.
3. *The Western Island*, OUP Pbk 1985, 15.
4. P. Corish, *The Irish Catholic Experience*, Dublin: Gill & Macmillan 1985, 2.
5. J. Duffy, *Patrick in his own Words*, Dublin: Veritas 1975, par. 10.
6. Ibid. par. 5.
7. See S. Kealy, *Soundings in Irish Spirituality*, Dublin: Carmelite Centre of Spirituality 1983, 23.
8. S. Kealy, Op. cit., 60, note 16.
9. J. Hennig, 'The Literary Tradition of Moses in Ireland', *Traditio* 7 (1949-51) 233-61, 253 here cited.
10. P. Corish, op. cit., 4.
11. D. Ó Corráin and F. Maguire, *Gaelic Personal Names*, Dublin: Academy Press 1981, 152.
12. See M. Curran, *The Antiphonary of Bangor*, Dublin: Irish Academic Press 1984, Ch. 3.
13. J. J. O'Meara, Gerald of Wales: *The History and Topography of Ireland* (Penguin Classics 1982, 81ff).
14. J. F. Kenney, *The Sources for the Early History of Ireland: Ecclesiastical*, N.Y.: Octagon/Dublin: Ó Táilliúir 1979, 358.
15. See Migne, *Patrologia Latina*, Vol. 72, cols 775-90; cited as Cog + col.
16. L. Bieler, *The Patrician Texts in the Book of Armagh*, Dublin 1979, 190.
17. Cog 778B.   18. Cog 781I.   19. Cog 788B-D.
20. R. Sharpe, 'Vitae Brigitae—Oldest Texts', *Peritia*, 1982, 89.
21. Cog 786A.   22. Cog 782C.   23. Cog 790C.
24. K. Hughes, 'On an Irish Litany of Pilgrim Saints', *Analecta Bollandiana* 77 (1959), 305-31, 319 here cited.
25. Cog 790C.
26. J. J. O'Meara, op. cit., 82.
27. C. Plummer, *Vitae Sanctorum Hiberniae*, Vol. 1, OUP 1968, 234f.
28. Ibid., 238.   29. Ibid., 242.   30. Ibid., 244.
31. Ibid., 239.   32. Ibid., 243, 245.
33. D. Ó Corráin and F. Maguire, op. cit., 110.
34. C. Plummer, op. cit., 249.
35. Ibid., 255.   36. Ibid., 250ff.   37. Ibid., 245ff.   38. Ibid., 248.
39. Ibid., 245, 257.

40. See K. Hughes, 'The Changing Theory and Practice of Irish Pilgrimage', *The Journal of Ecclesiastical History,* vol. XI (Oct. 1960), 143-57.

41. *Conf.,* par. 37.

42. B. Bischoff, 'Turning-Points in the History of Latin Exegesis in the Early Middle Ages', in M. McNamara, ed., *Biblical Studies,* Dublin: Dominican Publications 1976, 93-4.

42a See K. Hughes, op. cit. (note 24).

43. Migne, *Patrologia Latina,* 35:2149ff.

44. Old Irish Life of Columba in Whitley Stokes, *Lives of Saints from the Book of Lismore,* Oxford 1890, 168-81.

45. Stokes, op. cit., 169. See also D. Ó Laoghaire, 'Irish elements in the Cathechesis Celtica', in *Ireland and Christendom,* ed. P. Ní Catháin and M. Richter, Stuttgart: Klett-Cotta 1987, 151.

46. Stokes, op. cit., 20, 168.   47. Ibid., 170.   47a. Ibid., 171

48. A. and M. Anderson, *Adomnan's Life of Columba,* London: Nelson 1961, 503.

49. G.S.M. Walker, *Sancti Columbani Opera,* Dublin: Institute for Advanced Studies 1970, 57:23, 63:12, 79:1, 127:27, 137:23 (page and line indicated).

50. Ibid., 29:7.   51. Ibid., 27:1; 29:18.   52. Ibid., 35:27.

53. Ibid., 57:29.   54. Ibid., 63:12.   55. Ibid., 65:28.   56. Ibid., 79:1.

57. *Insight,* N.Y.: Harper & Row 1978, xxviii.

58. G.S.M. Walker, op. cit., 127:27, 137:23. See also C. Plummer, *Vitae Sanctorum Hibernaie,* Vol. II, OUP 1968, 254f., and chs iv, vi, ix.

59. Walker, op. cit., 63:13.

60. Ibid., Sermon 5.   61. Ibid., Sermon 4.   62. Ibid., Sermons 8-10.   63. Ibid., 87:25.

64. Ibid., 45:11, 18, 43:6 (Letter 5).

65. J. Carney, *Medieval Irish Lyrics* (Dublin: Dolmen Press 1985, 81-2, xix.